I0756195

IN THE ARENA

IN THE ARENA

Leading Building and Fighting the Good Fight

Ryan Nelson Holt

RNH Media

Published by RNH Media LLC

rnh.media

First Edition, 2026

Printed in the United States of America

To my father, Jim Holt. (39)

I hated you most of my life,

but God saved us both,

and now I am honored to be your son.

To all my brothers from other mothers,

thank you.

And to every man standing in the arena right now,

wondering if it's worth it.

It is.

Contents

Introduction

You picked up this book because something is off. You may not be able to name it precisely, but you feel it. The distance between the man you present and the man you actually are. The gap between your Sunday convictions and your Monday decisions. The quiet suspicion that you have been circling something important for a long time without ever stepping into it.

* * *

I want to be honest with you about what this book is and what it is not.

It is not a self-help book. It does not promise that the right morning routine will save your marriage or that a better mindset will fix what is broken in you. The men who need this book have usually tried those things. They know the difference between information and transformation, and they are tired of collecting the first while the second stays out of reach.

It is not a prosperity gospel in a different wrapper. I am not going to tell you that faithfulness guarantees ease, that obedience produces a comfortable life, or that God owes you good outcomes for your good behavior. He doesn't. The arena is hard. That is the point.

What this book is, as plainly as I can say it, is a field guide for men who are serious about the gap between who they are and who they are called to be. It is theological and practical in equal measure, because one without the other produces either a man who thinks well but acts poorly, or a man who works hard but drifts from any anchor. The Thinking Christian Operator, the man this book is written for, needs both.

* * *

The chapters ahead follow the actual sequence of formation: who you are before what you do, the internal before the external, the foundation before the building. We begin with identity, because every other discipline either rests on a solid identity or eventually collapses without one. We move through confession, fear, intentionality, habits, accountability, commitment, temptation, and emotional control. We end with a manifesto, not a motivational slogan, but a code. Something to return to when the fight gets long and the feelings stop cooperating.

Each chapter can stand alone, but they are strongest read in order. The disciplines build on each other the way floors of a building depend on what is below them.

* * *

A word about my authority to write this. I am not a pastor. I am not a theologian with credentials after my name. I am a man who has been in the forge: twenty-one years of sobriety, dialysis three days a week, a career built under constraint rather than ideal conditions. I have failed at most of what this book addresses. I have also gotten back up, repeatedly, and I know what that actually requires.

My authority comes from having been in the arena and still fighting the Good Fight. I am not writing from the stands about a fight I watched someone else fight. I am writing from inside it, with the dust and the blood to prove it. If that is the kind of voice you are looking for, this book is for you.

* * *

Wisdom is still calling from the city gates. She has been calling since before you picked up this book. You sensed it, or you would not be here. The question she is waiting to hear answered is not whether you understand what she is saying. It is whether you will step forward.

Turn the page. Let's get to work.

Ryan Nelson Holt

CHAPTER ONE

In The Arena

"It is not the critic who counts; not the man who points out how the strong man stumbles, or where the doer of deeds could have done them better. The credit belongs to the man who is actually in the arena."

Theodore Roosevelt

* * *

I remember the exact moment I understood what the arena meant.

I was thirty-seven years old, standing in a hospital room at two in the afternoon. My father had just been diagnosed with a disease that would take him in the next five years. My relationships were fracturing under the weight of years of neglect, my neglect. The business I'd built was hemorrhaging money because I'd been too proud to ask for help and too distracted to see the problems until they were crises. And in that concrete cavern, surrounded by the hum of fluorescent lights and the distant beeping of machines keeping strangers alive, I had nowhere left to hide.

For years, I had been performing the role of a man who had it together. I knew the right things to say. I attended the right events, shook the right hands, and projected the right image. But standing there in that room, I realized I had been watching my own life from the stands. Commenting on it. Critiquing it. Making plans for someday. Meanwhile, the actual arena of my existence had been left unattended.

My father was dying, and I hated him most of my life. I was desperately lonely, but I hadn't noticed. My company was failing, and I'd been too busy trying to look successful to do the hard work of actually succeeding.

That day, I didn't have a dramatic conversion. There was no voice from heaven, no sudden clarity. There was only a choice, the kind of choice that doesn't feel like much when you make it but changes everything that comes after. I decided to stop being a spectator in my own life. I decided to step into the arena.

What the Arena Actually Is

When I talk about the arena, I'm not offering you another piece of motivational language to add to your collection. I'm not talking about performance culture or grinding harder or optimizing your morning routine. The arena is something far more uncomfortable than any of that.

The arena is the place where your decisions reveal who you actually are. It's the space between intention and action, between what you say you believe and how you actually live. It's the conversation with your spouse that you've been avoiding for months. It's the financial reckoning you've been pushing off. It's the calling you've sensed but haven't had the courage to pursue. It's every moment where doing the right thing costs you something and doing the easy thing costs you more, just not right away.

Most men spend their lives circling the arena without ever stepping in. They know it's there. They can describe it in detail. They have opinions about what other men should do once they're inside. But when it comes to their own entry, there's always a reason to wait. The timing isn't right. The circumstances aren't ideal. They need more preparation, more resources, more certainty.

This is the myth of "someday" the quiet lie that convinces men they have unlimited tomorrows to get serious about their lives. Someday I'll have that conversation. Someday I'll make that change. Someday I'll become the man I know I'm supposed to be.

But the arena doesn't wait for someday. Neither does God.

The Wisdom That Calls Men Forward

The book of Proverbs opens with a striking image. Wisdom is personified as a woman standing in the public square, calling out to anyone who will listen. She doesn't whisper from a comfortable corner. She positions herself at the city gates, in the busiest intersections, in the places where life is happening and decisions are being made.

> ***"Out in the open wisdom calls aloud, she raises her voice in the public square; on top of the wall she cries out, at the city gate she makes her speech." (Proverbs 1:20-21)***

Notice where wisdom positions herself: not in the library, not in the monastery, not in the quiet places of theoretical contemplation. She stands in the arena of daily life: the marketplace, the city gate, the places where commerce and conflict and human struggle converge.

Wisdom isn't interested in men who merely think about living well. She calls out to men who are willing to act.

And notice what she offers. A few verses later, she makes her promise:

"If you turn at my reproof, behold, I will pour out my spirit to you; I will make my words known to you." (Proverbs 1:23)

The condition is clear: "if you turn." Wisdom requires a response. It demands movement, decision, action. God doesn't shape passive men. He shapes men who turn toward His voice, who step out of the stands and into the arena where His wisdom can actually reach them.

Throughout Proverbs, this pattern repeats. The wise man is never described as someone who merely possesses knowledge. He is described by his actions. How he handles money. How he treats his wife. How he responds to correction. How he conducts his business, how he raises his children. Wisdom, in the biblical framework, is not a set of ideas you hold. It is a way of life you practice.

"The fear of the Lord is the beginning of knowledge, but fools despise wisdom and instruction." (Proverbs 1:7)

The fool isn't defined by ignorance. The fool is defined by despising instruction, by refusing to be shaped, corrected, and refined. The fool stays in the stands where no one can challenge him. The wise man enters the arena where God can do His work.

The Quiet Killer

If wisdom calls men into the arena, something else whispers for them to stay out. That something is comfort.

Comfort is patient. It doesn't demand immediate surrender. It's content to wait years, even decades, for a man to slow down, drift off course, and settle for less than he was made for. Comfort tells you that you deserve rest before you've done the work that earns it. It tells you that good enough is enough. It tells you that the hard conversations can wait, the difficult changes can be postponed, the arena will still be there tomorrow.

And comfort is half right, which is what makes it so dangerous. Rest matters. Sustainability matters. Not every moment needs to be a battle. But comfort becomes deadly when it graduates from a rhythm of recovery to a permanent residence, when rest becomes avoidance, when taking a break becomes never starting again.

I've watched men sacrifice their marriages to comfort, choosing the path of least resistance until they looked up and realized their wives had become strangers. I've watched men sacrifice their health to comfort, their integrity to comfort, their calling to comfort. I've done it myself. Comfort never builds anything worth handing to the next generation. It doesn't strengthen faith or develop character or create legacy. It just maintains, until eventually there's nothing left to maintain.

Every man who wants to lead, build, or leave something meaningful behind must make a fundamental choice: Will I chase comfort, or will I chase calling? The arena demands this decision. You cannot serve both.

The Arena as Mirror

Here is what no one tells you about stepping into the arena: it will expose you.

You can lie to people. We all do it, the small presentations of ourselves that sand off the rough edges and present a polished image. You can even lie to yourself, constructing narratives that cast your failures as circumstances and your avoidances as wisdom. But you cannot lie to pressure. When the weight comes down, when the decision must be made, when there's no more time to prepare and plan and position. You find out who you actually are.

The arena strips away pretense. Your fears show up. Your actual motives, not the ones you tell people about, but the real ones driving your behavior, become visible. Your discipline or lack of it becomes undeniable. Your convictions either hold under weight or collapse into convenience.

This is terrifying. It's supposed to be. But it's also one of the greatest gifts available to any man who wants to grow.

Because here's the truth: you cannot change what you cannot see. As long as you're managing appearances and avoiding pressure, you'll never know where you actually need to grow. The arena's exposure is the beginning of transformation. The man who refuses to be exposed is the man who refuses to be transformed.

"As iron sharpens iron, so one person sharpens another." (Proverbs 27:17)

Iron sharpening iron isn't a gentle process. It involves friction, heat, the removal of what's dull and useless. It happens through contact, through pressure, through the willingness to be shaped by forces outside yourself. The stands don't sharpen anyone. Only the arena does.

What It Will Cost You

I won't pretend that stepping into the arena is painless. It isn't.

You will lose people. Some relationships only survive because you've been small enough to keep them comfortable. When you start growing, when you start making difficult decisions, when you stop playing the role they've assigned you, some people won't come along. This is grief, and it's real, but it's not a reason to stay small.

You will lose illusions. The stories you've told yourself about why you haven't pursued your calling, why your marriage is struggling, why your character has these particular gaps, many of these stories will be revealed as the comfortable lies they always were. This is painful, but it's the pain of healing, not harm.

You will lose a version of yourself. The man who stayed small to make others comfortable, who avoided conflict to keep the peace, who chose the path of least resistance because it was easier, that man will have to die. And that death, strange as it sounds, is something to grieve even as you celebrate what comes after.

But here is what you gain: clarity about who you are and what you're called to. Courage that comes from having faced hard things and survived. Responsibility that gives your days weight and meaning. Spiritual strength forged in the fire of actual obedience rather than theoretical agreement. And perhaps most importantly, a life that aligns with God's purposes rather than your fluctuating emotions.

The arena forces you to become the man you've only pretended to be when life was easy. That man is worth more than everything you'll leave behind.

Warriors, Not Spectators

God has never been in the business of building spectators.

Look at the men He chose throughout Scripture. Abraham was called to leave everything familiar and walk into an unknown future. Moses was pulled from comfortable exile to confront the most powerful ruler on earth. David was anointed as a boy and then spent years being hunted, tested, and refined before taking the throne. Paul's conversion wasn't a ticket to easy living, it was the beginning of shipwrecks, imprisonment, beatings, and eventual martyrdom.

None of these men were called to watch. They were called to build, protect, lead, and endure. They were called into arenas that would expose them, test them, and transform them. And through that process, they became the men whose stories we still tell thousands of years later.

The same God who called them is calling you. Not to comfort. Not to ease. Not to the stands where you can critique the fight without engaging in it. He's calling you into the arena: the messy, uncomfortable, stretching, refining place where daily obedience does its slow and painful work.

"Fight the good fight of the faith. Take hold of the eternal life to which you were called." (1 Timothy 6:12)

Notice the language: fight the good fight. Not think about the good fight. Not plan for the good fight. Not have opinions about the good fight. Paul understood that faith is not a spectator sport. The good fight is fought in the tension between who you are right now and who God is calling you to become. That tension only exists in the arena.

The Starting Line Isn't Pretty

If you're waiting until you're ready to step into the arena, you'll wait forever.

No one enters as a finished man. You come in with scars from old battles and wounds you're still nursing. You bring doubts that wake you up at three in the morning and failures that still make you wince when you remember them. You carry regrets and unanswered questions and parts of your story that don't make sense yet.

Good. That means you're a man.

God doesn't ask you to be polished before you step in. He doesn't require that you have everything figured out, that your theology is airtight, that your habits are perfected. He asks for something simpler and harder: willingness. Willingness to be shaped by what you encounter. Willingness to be corrected when you're wrong.

Willingness to be strengthened through difficulty rather than protected from it. Willingness to be used for purposes larger than your own comfort.

Leadership begins the moment you stop waiting for permission and start taking responsibility. It starts when you stop saying "someday" and say "today." It starts ugly and uncertain and scared, and it starts anyway.

My first step wasn't glamorous. Standing in that hospital room, I didn't have a five-year plan or a clear vision. I had a decision: stop watching my life happen and start participating in it. Everything that's come since grew from that single, terrified, completely unglamorous decision.

God honors direction. Not perfection. Not certainty. Direction.

Why This Book Exists

You're reading these words because something in you recognizes that you were made for more than you're currently living.

Not more noise. Not more busyness. Not more productivity hacks and morning routines and optimized schedules. You know the difference between activity and purpose. You've probably filled your life with the first while sensing the absence of the second.

What you're looking for is alignment, the deep satisfaction of a life pointed in the right direction, where your daily actions connect to something larger than your immediate comfort. You're looking for truth that doesn't flinch when tested. You're looking for a faith that works in the arena, not just in the pew.

This book is my attempt to point toward that life. Not with shortcuts or formulas, but with the hard-won clarity that comes from having failed at this more times than I can count and getting back up anyway. The chapters ahead will walk through what it means to lead yourself first before trying to lead anyone else. We'll examine how to build things that last: marriages, businesses, legacies, faith. We'll confront the enemies that keep men stuck and the disciplines that set them free.

But none of it matters unless you're willing to enter the arena. The stands are full of men with opinions about how the fight should go.

The world doesn't need more critics. It needs more men willing to be bloodied in the pursuit of something worthy.

* * *

So here's the question that matters more than any other I could ask you:

What are you avoiding?

Not what you're busy with, you're probably busy with plenty. But what conversation have you been putting off? What decision have you been delaying? What call on your life have you been negotiating with instead of answering? What would change if you stopped being a spectator to your own existence and stepped into the arena where God can actually reach you?

You don't need to have it figured out. You don't need to see the whole path. You just need to take the first step, today, now, before the comfort sets back in and "someday" starts sounding reasonable again.

Wisdom is still calling from the city gates. The arena is still open. The question is whether you'll be among the men who enter it.

Turn the page when you're ready to find out.

CHAPTER TWO

Identity Before Strategy

"The Lord does not look at the things people look at. People look at the outward appearance, but the Lord looks at the heart."

1 Samuel 16:7

* * *

The business plan was flawless. I had spent three months on it.

Market analysis. Financial projections. Competitive positioning. Growth strategy. Every section was polished until it gleamed. I had consulted mentors, revised based on feedback, stress-tested the numbers. When I walked into that meeting with potential investors, I believed I was ready. I had the strategy. I had the vision. I had the presentation memorized down to my planned pauses for emphasis.

What I didn't have was the identity to carry any of it.

The meeting started well enough. I hit my marks, delivered my lines, projected confidence. But then came the questions, not about my spreadsheets or my market research, but about me. How had I handled failure in the past? What would I do if the first strategy didn't work? How did I make decisions under pressure? What kept me grounded when things got chaotic?

I stumbled. Not because I lacked answers, but because the answers I had were performances rather than truths. I had rehearsed what a confident leader would say without becoming a confident leader. I had studied the appearance of steadiness without cultivating actual steadiness. I had built an elaborate external structure on an internal foundation of sand.

I didn't get the investment. But I got something more valuable: I got exposed. And in that exposure, I finally understood what had been wrong with every venture I'd attempted up to that point. I had been obsessed with strategy while ignoring the strategist. I had refined my plans while neglecting the man who would have to execute them. I had confused having a vision with having the character to see it through.

That day, I learned a lesson that has shaped everything since: identity comes before strategy. Always. And any man who reverses that order is building a house he won't be able to live in.

The Gap Where Potential Dies

Every leader wants a strategy. Strategies feel productive. They give you something to do, something to optimize, something to present to others as evidence that you're serious about your goals. The leadership industry has made billions selling strategies, frameworks, systems, methodologies, step-by-step blueprints for success.

But here's what no one wants to talk about: most strategies fail not because they're bad strategies but because the men carrying them can't hold the weight. The plan was sound. The execution collapsed. And it collapsed because execution is never just about tactics, it's about the character, discipline, and internal coherence of the person doing the executing.

You can stack plans, goals, frameworks, and tactics as high as you want. But if the man holding them is fractured by unresolved conflict, driven by unexamined insecurity, undisciplined in the small things no one sees, or unclear about who he actually is and what he actually believes, nothing sticks. The weight will find the weakness. It always does.

This is the gap where most potential dies. Not in the absence of opportunity but in the absence of readiness. Not in the lack of a good plan but in the lack of a good man to carry it. The gap between who you present yourself to be and who you actually are is the exact space where your ambitions go to die.

Identity always shows up. It shows up in how you handle criticism. It shows up in what you do when no one is watching. It shows up in the promises you keep and the ones you quietly abandon. It shows up in your marriage, your friendships, your finances, your health. Every arena of your life eventually reflects the man you've become, not the man you've marketed yourself as, but the man you've actually built through thousands of small choices.

Strategy only works when identity can carry it. This isn't a motivational platitude. It's an operational reality that will determine whether your plans amount to anything or collapse under the weight of who you really are.

Character Always Leaks

You can't outrun your internal reality. I've tried. Most men have. We believe we can compartmentalize. Be one man at work, another at home, a third at church, a fourth when no one's watching. We think we can contain our weaknesses to the areas where they won't matter, present our strengths in the areas where they will, and manage the whole performance indefinitely.

It doesn't work. Character is not compartmentalizable. Eventually, who you are leaks into everything you touch. Your private thoughts shape your public decisions. Your hidden habits determine your visible results. The man you are when no one is looking is the man who shows up when everyone is watching, no matter how good the mask.

If you're inconsistent in private, your results will eventually become inconsistent in public. If you avoid hard truths in your own mind, you'll avoid the hard truths your business or family needs to hear. If you compromise when the stakes feel low, you'll compromise when the stakes are high, because compromise is a muscle, and you've been training it. If you're ruled by your emotions at home, your leadership at work will be unstable no matter how professional you appear in meetings.

Identity isn't a personality trait you can adjust. It's not a setting you can toggle depending on context. It's the engine underneath everything else, the core operating system that runs every application of your life. And if the engine is broken, it doesn't matter how good your apps look on the screen. Eventually, the whole system crashes.

This is why dealing with the man behind the public version of yourself isn't optional self-help work. It's the most strategic thing you can do. Every hour you spend building your character will pay dividends in every arena of your life. Every hour you spend polishing your image while ignoring your soul is borrowed time that will come due with interest.

The Hidden Years

When Samuel arrived at Jesse's house to anoint the next king of

Israel, he wasn't looking for David. No one was. David was so far off the radar that his own father didn't think to bring him in from the fields. Jesse paraded seven sons before the prophet, each one apparently more kingly than the last, tall, strong, impressive in all the ways that seemed to matter.

But God wasn't looking at what Samuel was looking at.

"The Lord does not look at the things people look at. People look at the outward appearance, but the Lord looks at the heart." (1 Samuel 16:7)

When David finally arrived, the youngest, the forgotten one, the shepherd boy with sheep dung on his sandals, Samuel knew immediately. This was the one. Not because of his appearance or his credentials, but because of something God could see that the room could not.

But here's the part of David's story that gets skipped over: the anointing wasn't the coronation. Between the oil on his head and the crown on his brow lay more than a decade of formation. Years of running from Saul. Years of hiding in caves. Years of leading a ragged band of malcontents and outcasts. Years of learning to wait on God's timing when taking matters into his own hands would have been so much easier.

Twice, David had Saul at his mercy, the man who was hunting him, trying to kill him, standing between him and the throne he'd been promised. Twice, David's men urged him to take the obvious opportunity. And twice, David refused. Not because he lacked the ability, but because he had built an identity that wouldn't let him take a shortcut to his calling.

"The Lord forbid that I should do such a thing to my master, the Lord's anointed."
(1 Samuel 24:6)

David understood something that most ambitious men miss: the way you get to your calling matters as much as whether you get there. An identity built on shortcuts will produce a leadership riddled with compromise. A crown seized by force will sit uneasy on the head that wears it. God wasn't just preparing a throne for David; He was preparing David for the throne. And that preparation couldn't be rushed.

This is the pattern throughout Scripture. God builds the man before He builds the mission. Moses spent forty years in the wilderness learning humility before God sent him back to Egypt. Joseph spent years in prison learning faithfulness before Pharaoh elevated him. Paul spent years in obscurity after his conversion before he became the apostle to the nations. In each case, God wasn't being slow, He was being thorough. He refused to give these men influence that their identities couldn't hold.

God loves you too much to let your gift destroy you. And your gift will destroy you if it arrives before your character can carry it. This is grace, not punishment, the grace of a Father who knows that premature elevation leads to devastating collapse.

Formed in the Shadows

The arena may be public, but the man who steps into it is formed in the hidden places.

What David did in those caves while Saul hunted him, the prayers he prayed, the songs he wrote, the choices he made when no one but God was watching. That's where his identity was forged. By the time he took the throne, the real work was already done. The public coronation was just the revelation of a private formation that had been years in the making.

This is true for every man. Your identity is built in the shadows, in your thoughts when you're alone, in your discipline when no one is checking, in your private choices that will never make it to anyone's highlight reel. It's built in how you handle temptation when giving in would be easy and no one would know. It's built in

your willingness to tell yourself the truth when a comfortable lie would feel so much better. It's built in whether you obey God when obedience costs you something and disobedience would cost you nothing visible.

The world sees your results. God sees your process. The world evaluates your achievements. God evaluates your character. And character is forged almost entirely in the moments no one else sees.

This is why private discipline matters infinitely more than public performance. You can fake performance. You cannot fake the man who shows up when the performance is over. You can project confidence in a meeting. You cannot project genuine confidence into your own soul when you're lying in bed at night knowing the gap between who you pretend to be and who you are.

By the time the world sees you, the real work is already done, or it isn't. And if it isn't, no strategy will save you. The hidden man will be exposed. He always is.

The Mask That Suffocates

Most men don't lack an identity. They have the wrong one.

Over years of adaptation, self-protection, and social survival, you've built a version of yourself that isn't really you. It's a performance. A carefully constructed persona designed to earn approval, avoid rejection, and navigate the expectations of everyone around you. The mask fit well enough when you were younger. It may have even served you. But now it's suffocating you, and you're not sure anymore where the mask ends and you begin.

False identity takes many forms. For some men, it's the image of having everything together, the competent one, the one who doesn't need help, the one who's always fine. For others, it's the likeable one, the man who never makes waves, never says the hard thing, never risks disapproval. For others still, it's the tough one: the man who doesn't feel deeply, doesn't get hurt, doesn't need connection.

Each mask serves a purpose: it protects you from being known. And being unknown feels safer than being known and rejected.

But here's the cost: the mask doesn't just hide you from others. It hides you from yourself. Wear it long enough, and you lose track of who's underneath. You make decisions based on what the mask would do rather than what you actually believe. You build a life that fits the persona rather than the person. And eventually, you wake up in a marriage, a career, a life that belongs to a man you never really were.

The work of identity isn't just building something new. It's first dismantling something false. It's having the courage to ask hard questions: Which parts of how I present myself are actually me, and which parts are performance? Which of my goals are my own, and which did I adopt to impress people whose approval I was chasing? Where have I been so busy being who others expected that I never discovered who God designed?

This dismantling is terrifying work. The mask has been protecting you for years, from rejection, from vulnerability, from the possibility that the real you might not be enough. Taking it off means risking all of that. But keeping it on guarantees something worse: a life built on a lie, a legacy that belongs to a fiction, an arena fought in by a man who never existed.

The Doorway of Honesty

If false identity is the disease, honesty is the beginning of the cure. Not the politeness we call honesty in everyday conversation, but the brutal, uncomfortable, searching honesty that pulls back every layer of self-deception and looks at what's actually there.

Most men avoid their own truth because it's uncomfortable. We've built sophisticated systems of self-justification that explain why our failures are circumstances, why our weaknesses are other people's faults, why our patterns aren't really that bad. We compare ourselves to worse examples to feel better. We focus on our intentions rather than our impact. We mistake explaining our behavior for actually changing it.

But the arena doesn't bend to comfort, and neither does transformation. You can't change what you refuse to name. You can't grow past what you won't acknowledge. You can't build a true identity on a foundation of denial.

Real honesty asks questions that make you squirm: Where am I actually weak, not where do I wish I were weak? Where am I inconsistent between what I say and what I do? What habits are quietly destroying my potential while I pretend they're not that serious? Where is pride costing me relationships, opportunities, growth? Where is fear, not caution, but actual fear, driving my decisions more than wisdom or faith?

These questions don't have comfortable answers. They're not meant to. They're meant to expose, and exposure is the prerequisite to transformation. The prophet Nathan didn't come to David with gentle suggestions, He came with a story that ripped the mask off and forced David to see himself clearly. And David's response, genuine brokenness, real repentance, is what allowed him to remain a man after God's own heart despite catastrophic failure.

"Create in me a pure heart, O God, and renew a steadfast spirit within me." Psalm 51:10

That prayer only becomes possible after honesty. David couldn't ask for a pure heart until he admitted his heart was corrupt. He couldn't request a steadfast spirit until he acknowledged his spirit had proven unsteady. Honesty is the doorway to transformation because it's the only way to know what actually needs transforming.

Built in the Ordinary

Identity isn't built in dramatic moments. It's built in repetition. We like to imagine that character is forged in crucible moments, the big decisions, the defining tests, the dramatic crossroads where heroes are made. And those moments do matter. But by the time they arrive, the outcome is largely determined by thousands of small choices that came before. The crucible doesn't create your character; it reveals what your daily decisions have already built.

The quiet, boring, uncelebrated moments are where real men are formed. The alarm goes off, and you either get up or you don't, and whichever you choose, you're training yourself to keep choosing it. You're tempted to cut a corner that no one will notice, and you either hold the line or you compromise, and whichever you choose, you're making the next choice easier. You're angry at your wife, and you either speak with restraint, or you let your words wound, and whichever you choose, you're shaping the man who will face that situation again tomorrow.

This is the unsexy truth about identity formation: it's mostly mundane. It's choosing obedience when you don't feel like it. It's maintaining discipline when motivation has evaporated. It's protecting your integrity when the shortcut is right there and no one would know. It's praying when panic would be easier. It's staying focused when distraction is a click away.

Every one of these choices is a vote for the man you're becoming. Cast enough votes in one direction, and that's who you are, not because of any single decision, but because of the accumulated weight of a thousand small ones. Identity is compound interest. The daily deposits may feel insignificant, but over years, they build into something that can carry enormous weight, or they build into something that crumbles at the first real test.

The Unshakable Source

Here is the deepest truth about identity: it only stabilizes when its source is unshakable.

If you draw your identity from success, you'll break when success leaves, and it always leaves eventually. Markets turn. Ventures fail. Seasons end. The man whose identity depends on winning will be destroyed by losing, and losing is not a question of if but when.

If you draw your identity from approval, you'll break when people turn on you, and they will. Opinions shift. Loyalties fade. The crowd that cheers today boos tomorrow. The man whose identity depends on being liked will be held hostage by whoever's opinion he's currently seeking.

If you draw your identity from performance, you'll break under pressure, because there's always more pressure, always a higher bar, always another performance required to maintain what the last one earned. The man whose identity depends on his output will exhaust himself trying to earn what was never meant to be earned.

Every identity source that depends on circumstances will fail when circumstances change. And circumstances always change. The only identity that holds is one anchored to something that doesn't shift.

That means your identity must be rooted in who God says you are, His workmanship, created for good works He prepared in advance. It must be rooted in what He designed you for, the unique purpose woven into your existence before you drew your first breath. It must be rooted in the character He commands you to build, not as a way to earn His love, but as a response to a love that's already been given. It must be rooted in the purpose He placed in you and the integrity He expects as you pursue it.

"For we are God's handiwork, created in Christ Jesus to do good works, which God prepared in advance for us to do."
(Ephesians 2:10)

When your identity is anchored here, it doesn't depend on your performance, because your value was established before you performed anything. It doesn't depend on others' approval, because the only approval that ultimately matters has already been given. It doesn't depend on success, because your calling isn't measured by outcomes but by faithfulness.

Everything else is noise. Loud noise, convincing noise, noise that can sound like truth if you're not careful, but noise nonetheless. A man with his identity anchored in God can lose everything temporal and remain standing. A man with his identity anchored anywhere else is always one loss away from collapse.

What You Reproduce

If identity only affected you, the stakes would be high enough. But identity doesn't stay contained. It reproduces.

Every leader wants to influence people. But influence is not the duplication of knowledge. You can transfer information through teaching, but what you actually reproduce in others is your identity. People follow who you are long before they follow what you say. They absorb your character before they absorb your content. They catch your way of being in the world regardless of what you explicitly try to teach them.

This is why the most important thing you can give your children is not the right information but the right example. They will become like you far more than they will become like your instructions. If you're steady, you create steadiness in those around you. If you're grounded, you cultivate grounded people. If you're reactive and emotional, you sow instability that will show up in everyone you lead. If you're double-minded, saying one thing while doing another, you create confusion that will ripple outward for generations.

Your life teaches even when your mouth stays shut. Your presence preaches a sermon no one can ignore. Your identity is constantly broadcasting, and people are constantly receiving, whether you intend it or not, whether you're aware of it or not.

This is the weight of identity work. It's not just about you becoming who you were meant to be. It's about the people watching, your spouse, your children, your employees, your friends, and what version of manhood you're modeling for them. Get your identity right, and you set others up to find theirs. Get it wrong, and you pass along the same fractures, insecurities, and compromises that have limited you.

The Foundation Before the Building

This is why identity comes before every strategy in this book.

In the chapters ahead, we'll talk about leading well, building wisely, fighting the battles that matter, and leaving a legacy worth remembering. But none of that matters if the foundation isn't set. You can't lead boldly if you don't know who you are. You can't build with conviction if you're shaped by unexamined insecurity. You can't fight the good fight if you're spending all your energy fighting yourself.

Identity creates alignment. When you know who you are, you know what to say yes to and what to say no to. You stop chasing opportunities that don't fit and start recognizing the ones that do. Your decisions become clearer because they flow from a settled center rather than a scrambling insecurity.

Alignment creates momentum. A man who knows himself doesn't waste energy on internal contradiction. He's not fighting his own doubts while trying to lead others. He's not undermining his strategy with self-sabotage. All of his force moves in the same direction because all of him is pointed the same way.

Momentum creates impact. The man with a settled identity and clear alignment has compounding power that the fractured man will never achieve. Every action builds on the last. Every relationship reinforces the others. Every year adds to what came before rather than starting over from scratch.

Before you build anything, fix the man who will do the building. Before you enter the arena, make sure you know who's stepping in. The strategy will come. But the strategy can wait until the foundation is ready to hold it.

* * *

Identity work is uncomfortable. It requires looking at things you've spent years avoiding. It demands honesty when self-deception would be so much easier. It means dismantling masks you've grown attached to and building something true in their place.

But this is holy ground. The work of becoming who God designed you to be is the most sacred project you'll ever undertake. It's the work that makes all other work possible. It's the foundation that holds everything you hope to build.

So, here's the question I want you to sit with before moving on:

Where is the gap between who you present and who you are?

Not the gaps you're comfortable admitting, the small weaknesses you've already made peace with. But the real gaps. The inconsistencies that keep you up at night. The masks you've worn so long you're not sure what's underneath. The places where you know your character hasn't caught up to your calling.

Name them. Not to me, not to anyone else, but to yourself and to God.

Because you cannot change what you refuse to acknowledge. And the man you're meant to become is waiting on the other side of that honesty.

When the man is built, the mission becomes clear. When the mission is clear, the strategy becomes simple. But it starts here, with the unsexy, uncomfortable, life-changing work of becoming someone whose identity can carry what God has planned.

Identity comes first. Everything else follows.

CHAPTER THREE

The Fight Within

"I do not do the good I want to do, but the evil I do not want to do, this I keep on doing."

Romans 7:19

* * *

I was winning everywhere except where it mattered most.

From the outside, everything looked like success. The business was growing. New opportunities were coming in. People would shake my hand after events and tell me how much my words meant to them. I had built something visible and by many metrics valuable, and I could point to it as evidence that I was the man I presented myself to be.

But late at night, when the lights went out and the deafening silence settled, I knew the truth. I was losing a war no one could see, and I was losing badly.

The anger I couldn't control would surface at home over things that didn't warrant it. A misplaced comment from my friends, a mess left by my roommate, a minor inconvenience that somehow triggered a response wildly disproportionate to the offense. I'd watch myself react and feel like a passenger in my own body, knowing this wasn't who I wanted to be but unable to stop it.

The thoughts I couldn't quiet would ambush me at random moments, old failures I'd never processed, comparisons to men who seemed to have it more together, anxieties about the future that spiraled into worst-case scenarios I couldn't escape. My mind was not a peaceful place. It was a battlefield where I was usually losing.

The habits I couldn't break would reassert themselves the moment stress arrived. The escapes I turned to when pressure mounted. The shortcuts I took when discipline felt too hard. The compromises I made that no one saw but I knew about, small erosions of integrity that I told myself didn't matter but that accumulated into a gap between my public image and my private reality.

I could stand in front of hundreds and speak about becoming the man God designed. But when I looked in the mirror alone, I saw someone who hadn't won the fight that mattered most. I was conquering rooms while losing to myself. And I was terrified that one day the internal collapse would become external and everyone would see what I already knew.

That fear, the fear of being exposed as a fraud, was itself part of the internal battle. And like most of the internal battle, I was fighting it alone, in secret, convinced that admitting the struggle would destroy everything I'd built.

I was wrong about a lot of things during that season. But I was most wrong about that.

The Battle No One Sees

Everyone talks about external battles. The challenges at work. The conflicts in relationships. The obstacles between you and your goals. These are real, and they deserve attention. But they're not the battles that determine your life.

You can conquer a room and still lose to yourself. History is littered with men who achieved enormous external success while their internal world was collapsing. Leaders who built empires but couldn't build self-control. Visionaries who inspired thousands but couldn't discipline their own appetites. Men who won the applause of the world and lost everything that actually mattered, their integrity, their families, their souls.

The external battles are loud. They demand attention. They come with clear opponents and visible stakes. But the internal battles are quiet, and quiet is more dangerous. The thoughts you refuse to examine don't disappear; they drive your behavior from the shadows. The temptations you think you control are controlling you in ways you've stopped noticing. The anger you bury doesn't dissolve; it ferments into bitterness that poisons everything you touch. The insecurities you pretend don't exist are shaping your decisions more than any strategic plan.

When you avoid the internal fight, you become predictable in the worst way, emotional when you should be steady, reactive when you should be thoughtful, unstable when consistency is required. But when you face it, when you engage the battle most men run from, you become something rare: a man who can be trusted with weight because he's learned to carry his own first.

God cares about who you are long before He cares about what you accomplish. He's far more interested in the state of your soul than the size of your platform. This is why the unseen battles matter infinitely more than the seen ones. The arena may be where your calling is fulfilled, but the fight within is where you become the man capable of fulfilling it.

A Battlefield Called the Mind

The Apostle Paul was arguably the most influential Christian who ever lived, a man who planted churches across the known world, wrote a significant portion of the New Testament, and shaped theology for two thousand years. If anyone had reason to project an image of spiritual victory, it was Paul.

And yet, in his letter to the Romans, he offers one of the most brutally honest confessions in Scripture:

> *"I do not understand what I do. For what I want to do I do not do, but what I hate I do... For I have the desire to do what is good, but I cannot carry it out. For I do not do the good I want to do, but the evil I do not want to do, this I keep on doing."*
> *(Romans 7:15, 18-19)*

Read that again. This is Paul, the apostle, the church planter, the theologian, admitting that he does what he hates and fails to do what he wants. This is a man at war with himself, describing the experience of internal conflict that every honest man recognizes.

Paul isn't describing a problem unique to him. He's describing the human condition after the fall, the reality that something in us wars against what we know to be right. He calls this the flesh, and he's clear about its nature: the flesh doesn't want discipline, obedience, sacrifice, or long-term faithfulness. It wants comfort, pleasure, shortcuts, validation, and escape. It wants what feels good now regardless of what it costs later.

In his letter to the Galatians, Paul makes the conflict even more explicit:

"For the flesh desires what is contrary to the Spirit, and the Spirit what is contrary to the flesh. They are in conflict with each other, so that you are not to do whatever you want." (Galatians 5:17)

This is the fight within. Not a single battle but an ongoing war between two opposing forces, the flesh pulling you toward destruction dressed up as freedom, and the Spirit pulling you toward life that requires dying to yourself first. Every day you wake up, these forces are already at war. Every decision you make is a vote for one side or the other.

Your thoughts shape your identity, your courage, your obedience, yourself-control. Your mind is not neutral territory; it's the primary battleground where the war is won or lost. As Proverbs puts it, "As a man thinks in his heart, so is he." Your life is downstream from your thought life. Your actions follow your attention. Your character emerges from the thousands of mental choices you make about what to dwell on, what to believe, and what to rehearse.

This is why Paul urges believers to be transformed by the renewing of their minds. The battlefield is between your ears, and what happens there determines everything that happens everywhere else.

The Weapons of the Enemy

If the fight within is real, it's worth understanding the tactics of the enemy, because he has tactics, and they're devastatingly effective against men who don't recognize them.

The enemy rarely uses frontal assaults. He doesn't announce himself. Instead, he works through lies that feel like your own thoughts, accusations that sound like reasonable self-assessment, and suggestions that seem like wisdom. His primary weapons are not external temptations but internal narratives, the stories you tell yourself about who you are, what you're capable of, and what you deserve.

He whispers that you're uniquely broken, that your struggles are worse than other men's, that if anyone knew the real you they would be disgusted. He whispers that you've failed too many times to recover, that God's patience has limits and you've found them, that the damage is already done and trying to change now is pointless. He whispers that the temptation is too strong to resist, that this one compromise doesn't matter, that you can always start over tomorrow.

Notice the pattern: the enemy's weapons are never facts. They're interpretations. They take real experiences, your failures, your weaknesses, your struggles, and attach false meanings to them. The failure becomes evidence that you're fundamentally defective rather than a man in process. The weakness becomes proof that change is impossible rather than an invitation to depend on God's strength. The struggle becomes confirmation that you're alone in your brokenness rather than a common battle that men have been fighting and winning for generations.

The enemy also weaponizes isolation. He convinces you that your internal battles are shameful, that bringing them into the light would destroy you, that real men handle these things alone. This is one of his most effective tactics, because isolation creates the perfect conditions for the lies to grow unchallenged. Without other voices speaking truth, the enemy's whispers become the only voice you hear.

Finally, the enemy weaponizes your emotions. He doesn't need you to believe a lie intellectually; he just needs to get you feeling something, fear, shame, anger, lust, despair, and then convince you that the feeling is reality. Emotions are real experiences, but they are not reliable interpreters of truth. You can feel hopeless while hope is fully available. You can feel alone while surrounded by people who would help if you let them. You can feel like a failure while actually being in the middle of growth. The enemy knows this, and he exploits it constantly

The Weapons God Provides

If the enemy has weapons, so do you. And yours are stronger, but only if you use them.

Paul describes the believer's armor in his letter to the Ephesians: the belt of truth, the breastplate of righteousness, the gospel of peace, the shield of faith, the helmet of salvation, the sword of the Spirit which is the Word of God. This isn't religious decoration. It's combat equipment designed for a real war.

Notice that truth comes first. The belt holds everything else together; without it, the armor falls apart. Truth is your foundational weapon because the enemy's primary tactics are lies. When a whisper tells you that you're hopeless, truth responds: "There is now no condemnation for those who are in Christ Jesus." When a suggestion says you can't change, truth responds: "I can do all things through Christ who strengthens me." When an accusation claims God has given up on you, truth responds: "He who began a good work in you will carry it on to completion."

Truth cuts through emotional noise. When your feelings are screaming lies, truth speaks a steadier word. When confusion swirls, truth provides a fixed point. When the internal battle is at its most chaotic, truth anchors you to reality, not the reality your emotions suggest, but the reality God declares.

But truth requires discipline to deploy. A weapon left on the ground doesn't help you in battle. This is why Scripture memorization, regular time in the Word, and habitual reflection on what God says about reality aren't religious exercises for extra credit, they're training for war. The man who has truth stored in his mind can access it when the lies come. The man who hasn't is left trying to fight with weapons he doesn't have.

"I have hidden your word in my heart that I might not sin against you." Psalm 119:11

The psalmist understood that the fight within is won by men who have done the preparation before the battle arrives. By the time temptation shows up, by the time the lies start whispering, by the time your emotions are hijacking your judgment, it's too late to start memorizing Scripture. The preparation happens in advance .

The discipline of truth pays off in the moments when discipline feels impossible.

Feeling Without Folding

One of the most important skills in the fight within is learning to feel without folding, to experience your emotions fully without letting them take command.

Your emotions are real. They matter. They're carrying information about your internal state that deserves attention. The man who suppresses his emotions entirely isn't winning the internal battle; he's just losing it differently, building up pressure that will eventually explode, creating blind spots where unexamined feelings drive his behavior without his awareness, and cutting himself off from the full humanity God gave him.

But emotions make terrible commanders. When they lead your decisions, your life becomes inconsistent, up one day, down the next, depending on what you happen to be feeling. When they drive your responses, you become reactive, acting out of the immediate impulse rather than considered wisdom. When they determine your direction, you become unstable, chasing whatever feels most compelling in the moment rather than building toward something that requires sustained effort.

The distinction is this: emotions are indicators, not commanders. They tell you what's happening inside, but they don't tell you what to do about it. Fear indicates that something feels threatening; it doesn't mean you should run. Anger indicates that something feels unjust; it doesn't mean you should lash out. Desire indicates that something feels appealing; it doesn't mean you should pursue it. The emotion provides data. Wisdom interprets the data and decides the response.

Self-control is not the absence of strong feelings. It's the ability to experience strong feelings without being controlled by them. This is a mark of spiritual maturity, the capacity to feel the full weight of your emotions while still choosing obedience over impulse. Paul lists self-control as a fruit of the Spirit because it's supernatural; it's not something you generate through willpower alone but something that grows as you walk with God.

Learning to feel without folding is not a one-time achievement. It's a daily practice. Every time you feel anger rise and choose a measured response, you strengthen the muscle. Every time fear whispers retreat and you step forward anyway, you build capacity. Every time desire pulls toward compromise and you hold the line, you become more capable of holding it next time. The fight within is won in these small victories, repeated until they become your default pattern.

The Power of Daily Surrender

Here is the counterintuitive truth at the heart of the fight within: you win by surrendering.

Not surrendering to the enemy, surrendering to God. Not giving up the fight, giving up the illusion that you can win it in your own strength.

Paul, after describing his internal war in Romans 7, asks the desperate question: "Who will rescue me from this body that is subject to death?" And then he answers himself: "Thanks be to God, who delivers me through Jesus Christ our Lord." The rescue doesn't come from trying harder. It comes from a Deliverer.

Surrender isn't weakness. It's alignment. It's the daily decision to say: "Not my will, but Yours. Not my wisdom, but Yours. Not my strength, but Yours." This isn't passive resignation; it's active dependence. It's the recognition that the power to win the internal battle doesn't originate in you, it comes through you as you stay connected to the Source.

"I have been crucified with Christ and I no longer live, but Christ lives in me. The life I now live in the body, I live by faith in the Son of God, who loved me and gave himself for me." (Galatians 2:20)

Paul found victory not by fighting harder in his own power but by dying to himself and letting Christ's power flow through him. This is the paradox of the fight within: you win by admitting you can't win alone. You gain strength by acknowledging your weakness. You find freedom by submitting to a Master.

Daily surrender means starting each morning with an acknowledgment that you need help, that the day ahead contains battles you cannot fight in your own strength. It means returning to that posture every time you feel yourself taking back control, grabbing the reigns, trying to manage through willpower what requires grace. It means ending each night by bringing your failure to God rather than hiding them, trusting His forgiveness rather than your performance.

You don't win the internal battle once. You win it daily, through daily surrender. And each day's surrender strengthens you for the next day's fight.

The Fight Is Not Meant to Be Fought Alone

For years, I fought the internal battle in isolation. I believed that admitting my struggles would destroy my credibility, that real leaders handled these things privately, that bringing my inner war into the light would only expose me as a fraud.

I was wrong. And my isolation made everything worse.

The enemy loves isolation. It's the environment where his lies grow most effectively, because in isolation there's no one to challenge them. When you fight alone, every whisper sounds like truth because you have no other voices to compare it against. When you struggle in secret, shame compounds because you're convinced that no one else wrestles with what you wrestle with. When you hide your battles, they grow stronger in the dark.

James understood this:

"Therefore confess your sins to each other and pray for each other so that you may be healed." (James 5:16)

Notice the connection between confession and healing. There's something about bringing the hidden into the light, about speaking the shameful thing out loud to a trusted brother, that breaks its power. Sin thrives in secrecy. Shame feeds on isolation. But when you confess to another person, not to the whole world, but to someone trustworthy, you discover that the thing you feared would destroy you loses much of its grip.

The fight within is not meant to be fought alone. This doesn't mean broadcasting your struggles to everyone. It means finding a few men who can know you truly, who can hear your confession without running, who can speak truth when you're believing lies, who can hold you accountable without condemning you, who are fighting their own internal battles and understand the terrain.

This is why isolation is so dangerous and community is so essential. The man who has no one who knows his real struggles is the man most likely to fall. The man who has brought his battles into trusted relationship has already won a significant victory, he's refused to let shame keep him in the dark where it's strongest.

Finding this kind of community requires vulnerability, and vulnerability feels like weakness. But it's actually strength. It takes more courage to admit you're struggling than to pretend you have it together. The man who can say "I need help" is stronger than the man who maintains a facade while crumbling inside.

Victory Redefined

If you're waiting to win the internal battle completely before you consider yourself victorious, you'll wait forever. That's not how this works.

You will fail sometimes. You will take steps backward. You will slip in the areas you thought you'd mastered and struggle with patterns you thought you'd broken. There will be days when the enemy's lies feel louder than God's truth, when your emotions overwhelm your discipline, when surrender feels impossible and isolation feels safer than vulnerability.

This is not defeat. This is the nature of the fight.

Victory in the internal battle is not living without struggle. Victory is refusing to stop fighting. It's getting back up after every fall. It's returning to truth after believing lies. It's choosing surrender again after grabbing back control. It's confessing to your brother after isolating in shame. It's progress, not perfection.

Every time you step back into truth, you win. Every time you choose obedience over impulse, you win. Every time you silence a lie with Scripture, you win. Every time you stand back up after falling, you win. The enemy wants you to believe that failing means you've lost. But failing and staying down is losing. Failing and getting back up is winning, because you're still in the fight.

"For though the righteous fall seven times, they rise again." Proverbs 24:16

Notice that the righteous person is defined not by avoiding falls but by rising after them. The internal battle produces men God can trust, not because they never fail, but because they never stop fighting. Leaders who can withstand pressure because they've learned to withstand their own internal pressure first. Men who don't fold when the weight gets heavy because they've been practicing not folding in the privacy of their own souls.

The Man the Arena Requires

The arena is demanding. It requires clarity when confusion is easier. It requires strength when weakness feels safer. It requires consistency when inconsistency would be more comfortable. It requires a man who has learned to win invisible battles before he steps into public ones.

Chapter One invited you into the arena. Chapter Two established that your identity must be built before your strategy can succeed. This chapter has addressed what stands between you and that identity: the fight within that must be engaged before you can become the man your calling requires.

The internal fight is not optional. It's not a side quest while you focus on more important things. It's the main event. Every external battle you'll face in the arena is first won or lost in the invisible terrain of your thoughts, desires, emotions, and choices. A man who hasn't conquered himself will eventually be conquered by himself, publicly, painfully, and often at the worst possible moment.

But a man who has engaged the fight within, who has learned to deploy truth against lies, to feel without folding, to surrender daily, to fight in community rather than isolation, to define victory as progress rather than perfection, that man can carry weight. He can be trusted with influence. He can enter the arena and stay there when others retreat.

You don't lose to life. You lose to yourself. And you don't win in life until you win within. This is the hardest truth and the most liberating one: if the enemy is inside you, so is the battlefield where he can be defeated.

* * *

The fight within is the most important one you'll ever face. It's also the one you'll face every day for the rest of your life. There is no graduation, no final victory this side of eternity. There is only the daily engagement, the daily surrender, the daily choice to keep fighting.

So here's the question I want you to sit with:

Where are you losing the fight within, and who knows about it?

Not your theoretical weaknesses, but your actual ones. The thoughts that run on repeat when you're alone. The temptations that have become patterns. The emotions that are running your decisions more than you've admitted. The lies you've been believing so long they feel like truth.

And who knows? Who have you trusted with the real battle? Who is speaking truth when you're drowning in lies? Who is holding you accountable when no one else is watching? If the answer is "no one," you've identified the most urgent next step.

The fight within builds the man the arena requires. It's time to stop losing in secret and start fighting in the open, with God, with truth, and with brothers who won't let you fight alone.

The battle is real. But so is the power available to win it.

CHAPTER FOUR

The Power of Confession and Correction

"When I kept silent, my bones wasted away through my groaning all day long... Then I acknowledged my sin to you and did not cover up my iniquity. I said, 'I will confess my transgressions to the Lord' and you forgave the guilt of my sin."

Psalm 32:3, 5

* * *

I carried it for three years before I finally spoke it out loud.

The failure wasn't dramatic enough to make headlines or destroy my career. It was quieter than that, a pattern of compromise that had calcified into habit, a series of small deceptions that had grown into a false version of myself. From the outside, nothing looked wrong. But inside, I was slowly suffocating under the weight of what I refused to name.

I told myself the usual things. It wasn't that bad. Other people did worse. I could handle it on my own. God knew anyway, so what was the point of telling anyone else? These rationalizations kept me comfortable enough to keep hiding, but not comfortable enough to actually heal. The unconfessed thing sat in my chest like a stone, affecting everything without being addressed.

My relationships grew distant, though my loved ones couldn't have told you why. My leadership grew tentative, though my team wouldn't have identified the cause. My prayer life grew hollow, though I still showed up and said the words. The hidden thing wasn't destroying me all at once; it was eroding me slowly, stealing my peace by degrees, making me a diminished version of the man I was supposed to be.

Then came the morning when I finally confessed, not to God alone, but to a brother I trusted. We sat in his living room, and I spoke words I had rehearsed a hundred times in my head but never released into the air. I told him everything. Not the edited version, not the version that made me look slightly better, but the full truth.

And, the truth set me free.

What I expected was judgment, or at least disappointment. What I received was something I hadn't anticipated: relief. The moment the words left my mouth, the stone in my chest began to dissolve. My brother didn't flinch. He didn't lecture. He simply said, "Thank you for trusting me with that. Now let's figure out what needs to change."

That conversation, the confession and the correction that followed, changed the trajectory of my life more than any achievement, any strategy, any public success. In thirty minutes of honesty, I recovered something that three years of hiding had stolen: freedom.

I had discovered what I'm about to share with you: confession and correction aren't soft spiritual practices. They're disciplines for warriors. They're the difference between leaders who grow and leaders who collapse under the weight of their own blind spots. They're the tools God uses to rebuild men who've been broken by what they've hidden.

The Weight of What We Hide

David understood what hiding does to a man. In Psalm 32, he describes the experience with visceral honesty:

"When I kept silent, my bones wasted away through my groaning all day long. For day and night your hand was heavy on me; my strength was sapped as in the heat of summer." (Psalm 32:3-4)

This is the man who killed Goliath, who led armies, who was called a man after God's own heart, describing himself as wasting away, groaning, his strength sapped. Not because of external enemies but because of what he was carrying internally. The hidden sin was destroying him from within.

David's experience isn't unique. It's the universal human experience of unconfessed sin, and every honest man recognizes it. Hidden things don't stay small. They grow. Hidden sin grows shame that compounds with every day you don't address it. Hidden pride grows blindness that makes you increasingly unable to see yourself clearly. Hidden insecurity grows instability that affects every decision you make. Hidden fear grows silence that prevents you from speaking the truth that could set you free.

What you hide eventually hijacks your life. It may not explode all at once, most hidden things don't. Instead, they drip. A small compromise becomes a habit. A habit becomes a pattern. A pattern becomes your character. And eventually, your character becomes your downfall. The thing you wouldn't confess shapes the man you become, and the man you become determines everything you build.

This is why God doesn't leave us in hiding. He's not intimidated by your truth, He already knows it. He's not shocked by your failures, He saw them before you committed them. He simply wants you to stop pretending, because pretending is killing you. The weight of unconfessed sin is a burden you were never designed to carry, and every day you carry it, you grow weaker rather than stronger.

In the arena, pretending will get you killed. You can't fight effectively when you're carrying hidden weight. You can't lead with authority when you're living in duplicity. You can't build something lasting when your foundation is riddled with unaddressed cracks. Honesty isn't just a virtue, it's a survival requirement.

Confession as Freedom

Most men treat confession like punishment, a humiliating admission of failure that they avoid as long as possible. This misunderstanding keeps countless men in bondage to things that could be broken in an afternoon.

Confession isn't punishment. It's release. It's where chains break. When you confess, the lie loses its power because lies thrive in darkness and die in light. The sin loses its grip because sin draws strength from secrecy and weakens when exposed.

The shame loses its voice because shame tells you that you're alone in your struggle, and confession reveals that you're not. The enemy loses his leverage because his primary weapon is accusation, and confession takes that weapon away, you can't be blackmailed by what you've already disclosed.

Confession isn't announcing your weakness. It's refusing to keep living under it. There's an enormous difference between carrying something hidden and bringing it into the light. The hidden thing controls you; the confessed thing is something you've begun to control. The hidden thing defines you; the confessed thing becomes part of a story of transformation. The hidden thing isolates you; the confessed thing connects you to others who understand the struggle.

David discovered this. After his season of hiding, he finally confessed:

"Then I acknowledged my sin to you and did not cover up my iniquity. I said, 'I will confess my transgressions to the Lord' and you forgave the guilt of my sin."
(Psalm 32:5)

Notice the sequence: acknowledgment, uncovering, confession, forgiveness.

David stopped hiding, brought the truth into the light, spoke it to God, and received what hiding could never provide: the forgiveness of guilt. The weight that had been wasting his bones was lifted. The strength that had been sapped was restored. The groaning gave way to freedom.

This is what confession offers every man willing to practice it: not humiliation, but liberation. Not weakness exposed, but chains broken. Not failure announced, but freedom declared.

The Two Directions of Confession

Confession has two essential dimensions, and both matter. The first is vertical: confession to God. The second is horizontal: confession to trusted brothers.

Confession to God is where forgiveness originates. When you bring your sin to God, you're bringing it to the only One who can actually forgive it. First John makes this promise explicit: "If we confess our sins, he is faithful and just and will forgive us our sins and purify us from all unrighteousness." This vertical confession is essential, it restores your relationship with God, receives His forgiveness, and positions you to receive His cleansing.

But vertical confession alone is often not enough. This is why James adds another dimension:

> *"Therefore confess your sins to each other and pray for each other so that you may be healed." (James 5:16)*

Notice what horizontal confession provides that vertical confession alone may not: healing. There's something about speaking your truth to another human being, someone who can look you in the eye, who can respond, who can walk with you through the aftermath, that brings a dimension of healing that private confession to God doesn't always accomplish. This isn't because God's forgiveness is incomplete; it's because we're designed for community, and sin has communal dimensions that require communal remedy.

Confession to God addresses your guilt before Him. Confession to a brother addresses the shame that keeps you isolated, the secrecy that gives sin its power, and the accountability that makes real change possible. Both are needed. A man who confesses only to God may receive forgiveness but remain stuck in patterns because no one knows, no one is watching, no one is walking with him. A man who confesses only to other men but neglects bringing his sin to God misses the forgiveness that only God can provide.

The arena requires both dimensions. You need the vertical relationship with God that grounds your identity and provides forgiveness. You need the horizontal relationships with brothers who know your real struggles and can help you fight.

The Practice of Confession

Understanding that confession is valuable is not the same as knowing how to practice it. Most men have little experience with confession outside of vague prayers that acknowledge general sinfulness. What does real confession actually look like?

First, confession requires specificity. "I've been struggling" is not confession; it's evasion. "I've been looking at pornography three times a week" is confession. "I haven't been my best" is not confession; "I've been lying to my wife about our finances" is confession. Vague acknowledgments don't break anything; they just create the illusion of honesty while preserving the hiding. Real confession means the specific sin, the specific pattern, the specific failure.

Second, confession requires choosing the right person. Not everyone deserves access to your confession. You're looking for someone who has demonstrated trustworthiness over time, who will hold what you share in confidence, who cares more about your soul than about their comfort in the conversation. You're looking for someone who won't use your confession against you later, who won't be scandalized into distance, who can hear hard things without flinching and respond with both truth and grace.

Third, confession requires courage to initiate. No one will drag the truth out of you. You have to choose to speak it. This means overcoming the fear that tells you the consequences of confession will be worse than the consequences of continuing to hide. That fear is almost always lying. The consequences of hiding, the slow erosion of integrity, the growing weight, the increasing distance from God and others, are almost always worse than the temporary discomfort of honest conversation.

Fourth, confession requires humility to receive the response. When you confess to a brother, you're inviting him to respond, and his response may include correction, questions, or observations you don't want to hear. If you're only willing to confess on your terms, receiving only affirmation and never challenge, you're not really confessing; you're managing your image. Real confession opens you to whatever response your brother offers.

Fifth, confession requires repetition. This isn't a one-time practice. It's a rhythm of life. The man who confesses once and then returns to hiding has missed the point. Confession becomes a regular discipline, not because you're constantly failing in dramatic ways, but because you're constantly walking in the light rather than the darkness, constantly bringing what's hidden into the open before it has a chance to grow.

The Gift Most Men Refuse

Confession naturally leads to correction, and here's where most men get off the train. Everyone wants growth. Almost no one wants to be corrected. But growth is correction. You cannot grow without being adjusted, challenged, and changed.

Correction is not criticism. Criticism tears down without building up; correction builds up through honest assessment. Criticism comes from those who want to diminish you; correction comes from those who want to develop you.

Criticism is rooted in contempt; correction is rooted in care. The difference isn't always in what's said, sometimes hard words are needed, but in the motive behind the words and the relationship from which they come.

Think of correction as calibration. A compass that's slightly off will lead you further and further from your destination the longer you travel. Correction is the adjustment that keeps you on course. It addresses your mindset when your thinking has drifted. It challenges your motives when self-interest has crept in. It confronts your habits when patterns have become destructive. It redirects your attitude when pride or fear has taken over.

Proverbs is relentless on this point:

> *"Whoever heeds life-giving correction will be at home among the wise. Those who disregard discipline despise themselves, but the one who heeds correction gains understanding." (Proverbs 15:31-32)*

Notice the stark language: the person who refuses correction "despises themselves." That sounds harsh until you understand what's being said. When you refuse correction, you're choosing to remain in patterns that are damaging you.

You're choosing blindness over sight. You're choosing stagnation over growth. You're choosing a smaller life because you're unwilling to hear the words that could enlarge it. In that sense, refusing correction is a form of self-destruction, and what isself-destruction but a form of self-hatred?

The barrier to receiving correction is almost always pride. Pride convinces you that you're fine as you are, that you don't need outside input, that you already know what you need to know, that you're the exception to principles that apply to everyone else. Pride delays growth until life breaks you, and life will break you if you refuse the gentler breaking that correction offers.

Humility, by contrast, is not weakness. Humility is accuracy. It's seeing yourself clearly enough to recognize that you have blind spots, that others can see things you can't, that your perspective is limited and benefits from outside input. A humble man advances faster than a proud man every time, because the humble man actually receives the correction that could change his trajectory.

Correction from the Right Sources

Not all correction is created equal. Correction from the wrong source can discourage rather than develop, wound rather than heal, break rather than build.

You need truth-tellers in your life, people who will say the hard thing because they love you too much to let you continue unchallenged. You need mentors who care more about your soul than your comfort, who are willing to make you uncomfortable in the short term to serve your development in the long term. You need brothers who don't flatter you, who aren't impressed by your accomplishments or intimidated by your position, who can speak to you as an equal in need of the same grace they need.

Correction from these sources develops you. Correction from the wrong sources, from critics who don't care about you, from cynics who tear down everyone, from people who are projecting their own issues onto you, often does more harm than good. Learning to distinguish between the two is part of growing in wisdom.

Here's a useful test: does this person have my genuine good in mind, or are they serving some other agenda? Have they earned the right to speak into my life through relationship and demonstrated care? Is their correction consistent with what I know to be true from Scripture and from other trusted sources? Am I resisting because they're wrong, or am I resisting because I don't want to hear what's right?

The last question is the hardest, because pride is skilled at disguising itself as discernment. Sometimes you reject correction because it's genuinely misguided. But often you reject it because it's genuinely accurate and you don't want to face it.

Learning to tell the difference requires the very humility that receiving correction develops, which means you have to start somewhere, trusting that God will grow your discernment as you practice the discipline.

A strong brotherhood gives you mirrors you can trust. Men who know you well enough to see your blind spots and love you enough to point them out. Men who have walked with you long enough to distinguish between who you are and who you're pretending to be. Men who will tell you the truth even when the truth is uncomfortable, because that's what real brothers do.

When God Himself Corrects

Beyond human correction, there's a deeper level: the correction that comes directly from God. And understanding how God corrects changes everything about how you receive it.

The writer of Hebrews addresses this directly:

> *"My son, do not make light of the Lord's discipline, and do not lose heart when he rebukes you, because the Lord disciplines the one he loves, and he chastens everyone he accepts as his son." (Hebrews 12:5-6)*

This passage addresses both errors men make when facing God's correction. The first is making light of it, dismissing divine discipline as coincidence, bad luck, or irrelevant. The man who makes light of God's correction misses the opportunity it represents. The second error is losing heart, receiving God's discipline as evidence of rejection, punishment, or abandonment. The man who loses heart misunderstands the nature of what's happening.

The truth is that God's correction is evidence of love. He disciplines the one He loves. He chastens everyone He accepts as a son. If you're experiencing God's correction, it's not because He's rejected you, it's because He's accepted you as His own. A father who doesn't correct his children doesn't really care about them. A father who corrects does so precisely because he cares about who they're becoming.

God's correction isn't harsh, it's precise. He's not trying to embarrass you or destroy you or make you feel small. He's removing what keeps you small. He's cutting away what keeps you stuck. He's strengthening what keeps you steady. His correction has one goal: making you into the man you were designed to be. Everything He removes is something that was getting in the way of that.

This reframe changes how you respond to difficulty. When you experience hardship that exposes weakness, that's correction. When circumstances force you to confront patterns you've been avoiding, that's correction. When doors close that would have taken you somewhere God didn't want you to go, that's correction. The question isn't whether God is correcting, He often is. The question is whether you're receiving it as the gift it is.

The Complete Cycle

Confession without correction is incomplete. You can confess all day long and never change if confession becomes merely emotional relief rather than the beginning of transformation.

Some men treat confession like a reset button they never follow through on. They confess, feel better, and then return to the same patterns, until they need to confess again. This creates a cycle of sin, confession, relief, sin, confession, relief that never leads to actual growth. Confession has become a way to manage guilt without ever addressing the root issue.

Real confession leads to real change. Real change requires correction. After you confess, the question becomes: what needs to be different? What thought patterns need to be renewed? What habits need to be broken or built? What accountability structures need to be put in place? What heart issues are driving the behavior that confession just exposed? Correction is the process of actually addressing these questions rather than just acknowledging that they exist.

God doesn't want apologies. He wants transformation. He's not interested in men who feel bad about their sin but never change. He's interested in men who bring their sin into the light and then do the work of becoming different. Confession opens the door; correction walks through it.

This is why confession to a trusted brother is so valuable, it builds in the correction naturally. When you confess to someone who cares about your growth, they're not going to simply say "thanks for sharing" and move on. They're going to ask questions. They're going to offer perspective. They're going to check in on you later. They're going to help you identify what needs to change and hold you accountable for changing it. The horizontal dimension of confession provides the context for correction that vertical confession alone often lack

The Warrior's Rhythm

Leaders stumble. This is not failure; it's the human condition. The question is never whether you'll fail, you will, but what you do after you fall.

Warriors have a rhythm: confess, correct, continue.

Confess quickly. Don't let sin grow roots. The longer you wait to confess, the deeper the shame grows, the heavier the weight becomes, the harder it is to finally speak. The enemy wants you to delay, because delay strengthens his position. Quick confession keeps short accounts with God and with others, preventing small failures from becoming entrenched patterns.

Correct immediately. Don't confess and then drift back to the same path.

Adjust your direction, your attitude, your habits, your behavior. Put accountability in place. Remove access to temptation where you can. Build new patterns to replace the old ones. Do the work of actually changing, not just feeling bad.

Continue boldly. This is the part most men miss. After confession and correction, many men walk in defeated hesitation, wondering if they've disqualified themselves, uncertain if they're still allowed to pursue their calling. But God's forgiveness is real, and restoration is the point. You're not meant to spend the rest of your life apologizing for failures you've already confessed. You're meant to receive God's restoration and continue the mission with renewed clarity and strength.

You don't lose ground when you fail. You lose ground when you hide. The man who fails, confesses, corrects, and continues is far more dangerous to the enemy than the man who appears to never fail but is hiding patterns that are slowly destroying him. Confession cleans your foundation. Correction strengthens your structure.

Continuing keeps you moving forward.

What the Arena Requires

You can survive with hidden sin. You just can't lead with it, not well, not sustainably, not with the authority that comes from alignment between your public words and your private reality.

You can build with pride. You just can't sustain anything with it. Pride builds walls that correction can't penetrate, and behind those walls, the slow decay continues unchecked.

The arena is full of pressure. You can't fight well when you're weighed down by what you're hiding. You can't lead with conviction when you know your life doesn't match your message. You can't build with confidence when you're constantly worried about exposure.

Confession clears your spirit. Correction stabilizes your soul. Together they make you the kind of man God can trust with influence, not because you're perfect, but because you're walking in the light. Your failures are known. Your patterns are being addressed. Your blind spots have people pointing them out. You're not pretending to be something you're not.

This is why God calls you to walk in truth, not to shame you, but to free you. The truth sets free. The hiding keeps you bound. The man who has learned to confess and receive correction walks lighter than the man carrying hidden weight. He has nothing to protect, nothing to maintain, no image to manage. He can focus entirely on the mission rather than splitting his attention between the mission and the exhausting work of keeping up appearances.

When you know how to confront your truth, nothing intimidates you, because you've already faced the hardest thing, which is yourself. When you know how to correct your course, nothing derails you permanently, because you've learned that every failure is just information for the next adjustment. When you know how to move forward after failure, nothing stops you, because you've stopped expecting perfection and started practicing progress.

That is the internal power of a man who has learned the disciplines of confession and correction. That is the stability required to remain in the arena when others retreat. That is the freedom God offers every man willing to walk in the light.

* * *

The stone I carried for three years dissolved in thirty minutes of honesty. That's not an exaggeration. The thing I thought would destroy me if I spoke it actually lost most of its power the moment it left my mouth. What followed, months of correction, accountability, and rebuilding, was hard work. But it was work done in the light, not hiding in the dark.

Confession and correction aren't punishments to be avoided. They're gifts to be practiced. They're the disciplines that separate men who grow from men who stagnate. They're the tools God uses to rebuild what hiding has damaged.

So here's the question I want you to sit with:

What are you carrying that needs to be confessed, and who will you tell?

Not the small stuff you're comfortable admitting, the real weight. The thing that came to mind as you read this chapter. The pattern you've been managing alone. The failure you've been hiding. The struggle you've convinced yourself no one can know about.

And who will you trust with it? Who has earned that access through demonstrated faithfulness? Who will hear you without flinching and help you walk toward change?

The weight doesn't have to stay. The chains don't have to hold. But

they won't break on their own. Confession breaks them. And the freedom on the other side is worth every uncomfortable moment it takes to get there.

The arena is waiting. You can enter it carrying weight, or you can enter it walking free. The choice is yours, and it starts with speaking what you've been hiding.

CHAPTER FIVE

Battling Fear, Doubt, and Comparison

"Have I not commanded you? Be strong and courageous. Do not be afraid; do not be discouraged, for the Lord your God will be with you wherever you go."

Joshua 1:9

* * *

I almost didn't make the call.

The opportunity was exactly what I'd been praying for, a chance to truly help people; that could change the trajectory of everything in my life. The chance had come unexpectedly, and all I had to do was confirm. Pick up the phone, say yes, and step into something I'd wanted for years.

Instead, I sat at my desk for three hours, paralyzed.

Fear started it. What if I wasn't ready? What if I got there and froze? What if my passion for helping others turned people off? What if this was the moment that exposed me as a fraud, someone who could talk about leadership but couldn't actually lead when it mattered?

Then doubt joined the assault. Maybe I'd misread the situation.

Maybe God wasn't actually opening this door, maybe I was forcing something that wasn't meant for me. Maybe my sense of calling was just ego dressed up in spiritual language. Who was I to think I had something worth saying to people who'd accomplished more than I had?

And then comparison delivered the finishing blow. I thought about the other men they could have hired, guys with better credentials,

more polished resumes. I scrolled through the company's registry and felt smaller with every name listed. They wanted me? There must have been a mistake. Or maybe I was a pity hire, a favor, someone to fill a seat they couldn't fill with someone better.

Three hours. That's how long I let fear, doubt, and comparison hold me hostage while an opportunity sat waiting for a simple yes. Three hours of my mind spinning through worst-case scenarios that existed nowhere except in my imagination. Three hours of questioning what God had made clear and measuring myself against people running entirely different races.

I eventually made the call. But it took a friend calling me on the phone, hearing the lack of confidence in my voice, and asking what was wrong. When I told him, he laughed, not mockingly, but with the recognition of someone who'd been in the same place. "You're negotiating with the enemy," he said. "Just make the call."

So I did. And the position became one of the defining life-altering changes I'd ever attempted. Not because I would perform perfectly, I definitely do not, but because I took a chance on myself and showed up despite the voices telling me not to. I've since learned that this is almost always how it works: the things that fear, doubt, and comparison try hardest to prevent are usually the things God most wants you to walk into.

These three enemies have been fighting me my entire adult life. They haven't stopped. I've just learned to recognize them, name them, and refuse to let them vote on my obedience.

The Quiet Assassins

Fear, doubt, and comparison are the quiet assassins of calling. They don't announce themselves with fanfare. They don't show up in obvious forms that you can easily identify and reject. They whisper. They suggest. They wear you down piece by piece until the man God designed gets buried under the man you've tolerated.

What makes these three so dangerous is their subtlety. Fear often masquerades as wisdom, surely it's just prudent to wait until conditions are better, until you're more prepared, until the timing is more certain. Doubt often sounds like humility, who are you to think God would use you, that your contribution matters, that you have anything worth offering? Comparrison often feels like legitimate assessment, if you're behind others in your field, isn't that just a fact you need to accept rather than a lie you need to reject?

But wisdom that paralyzes is not wisdom, it's fear in disguise. Humility that undermines obedience is not humility, it's doubt wearing a mask. Assessment that steals your peace and derails your calling is not honest evaluation, it's comparison doing its destructive work.

Every leader faces these three. Every man who steps into the arena confronts them. The difference between men who fulfill their calling and men who bury it isn't the absence of fear, doubt, and comparison, it's the refusal to let them rule. The strong feel these enemies and move forward anyway. The defeated feel them and stop.

Understanding how each operates is the first step to defeating them. They work together, often in sequence, but each has its own tactics, its own lies, and its own antidote.

The Enemy Called Fear

Fear is a liar with excellent timing. It rarely attacks when you're comfortable, settled, or playing it safe. Fear waits until you're stepping into purpose, until you're on the edge of something that matters, until obedience requires risk. Then it strikes.

Notice when fear shows up in your life. It appears at the threshold of calling, when you're about to make the ask, have the conversation, launch the venture, speak the truth, step into the arena. Fear's timing reveals its origin. It's not trying to protect you from danger; it's trying to prevent you from obedience. If fear only showed up when real threats emerged, it would be useful data. But fear shows up when God-ordained opportunities emerge, which makes it something else entirely: opposition.

Fear's primary tactic is imagination. It rarely deals in facts, it deals in possibilities. Fear paints a thousand failure scenarios in your mind, each more vivid than the last. You rehearse disasters that don't exist. You live as if your anxieties are prophecies rather than lies. Your mind becomes theatre where worst-case outcomes play on repeat, and you forget you're the one choosing to stay in the audience.

The failure scenarios fear presents almost never materialize. Think back over your life: how many of the things you feared actually happened? How many hours have you spent dreading outcomes that never arrived? Fear is powerful not because its predictions are accurate but because you feed it with imagination. You give it material to work with every time you dwell on what might go wrong instead of what obedience requires right now.

God's response to fear is not a suggestion, it's a command. When Joshua stood at the edge of the promised land, taking over leadership from Moses, facing enemies and obstacles he'd never confronted, God didn't offer gentle encouragement. He issued an order:

"Have I not commanded you? Be strong and courageous. Do not be afraid; do not be discouraged, for the Lord your God will be with you wherever you go." (Joshua 1:9)

This is not "try not to be afraid if you can help it." This is "do not be afraid" imperative, non-negotiable, a direct command. And the basis for the command is not Joshua's strength, not his track record, not his preparation. The basis is God's presence: "the Lord your God will be with you wherever you go."

The antidote to fear is not courage generated from within. It's presence, the awareness that you don't enter the arena alone. When you know God is with you, fear becomes noise rather than direction. It may still speak, but it no longer gets to vote on your obedience.

Courage, then, is not the absence of fear. Courage means fear doesn't get the final word. Fear can scream. Fear can shake you. Fear can present elaborate scenarios of everything that could go wrong. But courage drags fear into the arena and moves anyway. Courage is not emotional confidence, it's spiritual obedience. It's doing what God said to do regardless of what your feelings are saying.

The Enemy Called Doubt

Doubt is subtler than fear. Fear attacks your circumstances, what might happen, what could go wrong. Doubt attacks something deeper: your identity. Doubt doesn't say you can't do something; it says you're not the kind of man who can.

This distinction matters. Fear is about external outcomes; doubt is about internal reality. Fear says the situation is too dangerous; doubt says you're too deficient. Fear questions whether this specific endeavor will succeed; doubt questions whether you were ever meant to try. Doubt strikes at the foundation of who you understand yourself to be.

Doubt's lies often sound like these: Did God really call you to this? Are you sure you heard Him correctly? Maybe you're just projecting your own desires onto divine guidance. Maybe the sense of calling is ego, not anointing. Look at your track record, why would God use someone with your history? Doubt questions God's calling, God's timing, God's grace, God's strength, and eventually, if left unchecked, God's character.

But here's what doubt doesn't want you to notice: it's rarely actually about God. Doubt is about you not believing who God says you are. When you doubt your calling, you're not really doubting God's ability to call, you're doubting that He would call you. When you doubt His timing, you're not really questioning His sovereignty, you're questioning whether you deserve His attention. Doubt wraps itself in theological language, but at its core, it's an identity crisis.

One of the most honest prayers in Scripture comes from a father desperate for Jesus to heal his son. When Jesus tells him that everything is possible for one who believes, the father responds:

"I do believe; help me overcome my unbelief!" Mark 9:24

This is the prayer of a man who refuses to let doubt have the final word while being honest that doubt is present. He doesn't pretend he has no doubt, that would be dishonest. But he doesn't surrender to the doubt either, that would be defeat.

Instead, he brings the doubt to Jesus and asks for help. This is the model: acknowledge the doubt, refuse to be ruled by it, and bring it to the One who can overcome it.

Doubt collapses when truth steps in. This is why knowing what God actually says about you matters so much. When doubt whispers that you're disqualified, truth responds that there is no condemnation for those in Christ. When doubt suggests you're unequipped, truth responds that God who began a good work in you will carry it to completion. When doubt questions whether you're chosen, truth responds that you were selected before the foundation of the world.

Doubt is not evidence that you're weak. It's evidence that you're a man. Every man who has ever stepped into calling has wrestled with doubt. The question is not whether doubt will come but what you do when it arrives. Do you let it stop you, or do you bring it to the light and keep moving.

The Enemy Called Comparison

Comparison might be the most pervasive enemy of the three, especially in an age of constant visibility into everyone else's highlight reel. Social media has turned comparison into a daily assault, a continuous stream of other people's successes, milestones, and carefully curated achievements designed to make you feel behind, inadequate, and late.

Comparison is spiritual cancer. It metastasizes into every area of your life, eating away at contentment, clarity, and focus. It convinces you that everyone else is further ahead, more blessed, more favored, more successful, and that their advancement somehow diminishes your own standing. Comparison transforms brothers into competitors and fellow travelers into threats.

The lies comparison tells are predictable: You're behind. You should be further along by now. Look how much more they've accomplished. You're invisible while others are celebrated. God must favor them more than He favors you. Why hasn't your turn come when theirs came so easily?

And then comparison delivers its real damage: you stop running your race. You become so fixated on someone else's lane that you slow down in your own. You spend energy analyzing their success that should have gone toward pursuing your calling. You lose sight of what God assigned you because you're too busy watching what He assigned someone else.

Paul understood this danger and addressed it directly:

"We do not dare to classify or compare ourselves with some who commend themselves. When they measure themselves by themselves and compare themselves with themselves, they are not wise."
(2 Corinthians 10:12)

Notice Paul's verdict: comparison is not wise. It's not humble self-assessment.

It's not realistic evaluation. It's foolishness, a category error that judges your running by someone else's race. You cannot accurately measure your faithfulness by comparing it to someone else's outcomes, because you don't know their assignment, their resources, their season, or their struggles. You only see the visible results; you don't see the invisible context.

Jesus dealt with comparison directly in His conversation with Peter at the end of John's Gospel. After commissioning Peter for ministry, Jesus hints at the suffering Peter will face. Peter immediately looks at John and asks, "Lord, what about him?" Jesus' response is instructive:

"If I want him to remain alive until I return, what is that to you? You must follow me." (John 21:22)

In other words: John's assignment is not your concern. Your only job is to follow Me. Stop looking sideways at what I'm doing with someone else and focus on what I'm calling you to do. This is the antidote to comparison: clarity about your own calling so complete that other people's paths stop being relevant to yours.

Comparison disappears when identity is clear. When you know who God made you, what He gave you, the battles He assigned to you, the gifts He placed in you, and the pace He set for you, then other people's accomplishments stop feeling like threats. They become reasons for celebration rather than sources of envy, because you're not competing with people who aren't running your race.

The Unholy Alliance

What makes fear, doubt, and comparison so formidable is that they rarely operate alone. They work as a system, each feeding the others, creating a self-reinforcing cycle that can paralyze a man completely.

Here's how the cycle typically works: Comparison notices that someone else is succeeding where you haven't yet. Doubt uses that observation to question whether you're actually called to what you thought you were called to, after all, if you were really meant for this, wouldn't you be further along? Fear then catastrophizes the implications, if you're not called, if you're behind, if you're missing something others have, then any step forward risks exposing your inadequacy. The result is paralysis: you stop moving, stop trying, stop obeying.

The cycle can also begin at a different point. Fear of failure triggers doubt about whether you should even try. Doubt about your calling leads you to compare yourself to others who seem more certain, more confident, more blessed.

Comparison confirms that you're indeed lesser than you hoped. And back to fear you go, now with even more ammunition.

The enemy uses these three because they work. Fear freezes you. Doubt weakens you. Comparison distracts you. Together, they dismantle your confidence and your courage without ever delivering a direct blow. They don't need to destroy you outright, they just need to discourage you enough to stop moving. The enemy doesn't win when you fall. He wins when you stop getting back up.

Understanding the system helps you fight it. When you notice one of these enemies active in your mind, look for the others, they're usually nearby. And when you address one, you often weaken the others. Clarity about your identity defeats comparison, which removes the evidence doubt was using against you, which cuts off the scenarios fear was building.

The Weapons That Win

Fear, doubt, and comparison all share one critical weakness: they cannot survive a man who acts. They thrive in hesitation, contemplation, and delay. They wither when you move.

This is not to say that action alone defeats them, it doesn't. But action denies them the environment they need to grow. When you make the call, take the step, speak the truth, show up despite the voices telling you not to, the grip loosens. The lies begin to fall apart. The intimidation weakens. You don't think your way out of fear, doubt, and comparison. You move your way out.

But action needs to be grounded in something deeper, or it becomes mere willpower, and willpower eventually exhausts. The deeper grounding is truth. Each of these enemies operates through lies, and lies dissolve in the presence of truth.

Fear's lie is that danger is too great; truth responds that God is greater. Doubt's lie is that you're disqualified; truth responds that God's grace qualifies. Comparison's lie is that you're behind; truth responds that you're running a race no one else is running.

This means knowing Scripture matters enormously, not as academic exercise but as arsenal. When fear attacks, you need truths like "The Lord is my light and my salvation, whom shall I fear?" ready to deploy. When doubt whispers, you need truths like "I can do all things through

Christ who strengthens me" armed and available. When comparison steals your peace, you need truths like "We are God's handiwork, created in Christ Jesus to do good works, which God prepared in advance for us to do" locked in your memory.

Community also matters in fighting these enemies. Chapter Three established that the fight within isn't meant to be fought alone, and Chapter Four showed how confession and correction happen in trusted relationships. Fear, doubt, and comparison all grow stronger in isolation. Bringing them into the light with a brother who can speak truth breaks much of their power. The friend who called me on the phone and told me to just make the call did more in thirty seconds than my three hours of internal wrestling had accomplished.

Sometimes you need someone else to name the enemy for you. Sometimes you need someone else to remind you of truth you've forgotten. Sometimes you just need someone to stand with you and say, "I know this is hard, but you need to move." Brotherhood is a weapon against fear, doubt, and comparison that the isolated man doesn't have access to.

Replacing the Voices

The battle against fear, doubt, and comparison is ultimately won by replacing their voices with better ones. You cannot simply silence them through willpower,they'll return. You have to crowd them out with truth spoken so consistently that it becomes your default internal narrative.

Replace fear with faith. Not faith as a feeling, feelings are unreliable. Faith as a decision to trust what God has said over what your emotions are screaming. Faith as action taken in alignment with God's promises regardless of the fear still present. Fear may still speak; faith responds, "I hear you, but God's Word has more authority than your predictions."

Replace doubt with truth. This requires knowing truth deeply enough that it's accessible when doubt attacks. When doubt questions your calling, truth responds with specific promises God has made about His purposes for you. When doubt questions your adequacy, truth responds with specific declarations about God's power made perfect in weakness. Doubt withers when exposed to what God has actually said.

Replace comparison with identity. When you know who you are in Christ, not theoretically but as settled conviction, other people's success loses its power to destabilize you. You stop seeing them as competitors and start seeing them as fellow runners, each with their own lane, each with their own calling, each with their own race to complete. Your identity becomes so clear that comparison has nothing to hook into.

This replacement is not a one-time event. It's daily practice. Every morning, fear, doubt, and comparison will attempt to reassert themselves. Every morning, you choose which voices get your attention. Every morning, the battle is won or lost in the first moments when you decide whether to dwell on the lies or to rehearse the truth.

You don't need more confidence, confidence is just a feeling that comes and goes. You need more clarity: clarity about who God is, who He says you are, and what He's called you to do. Clarity is stable when confidence wavers. Clarity is available when feelings fail. Clarity is the foundation that holds when fear, doubt, and comparison throw their worst at you.

The Man Who Wins These Battles

A man who has learned to fight fear, doubt, and comparison becomes something formidable, not because these enemies stop appearing, but because they stop ruling.

A man who isn't ruled by fear is dangerous to the enemy's kingdom. He moves when others freeze. He speaks when others stay silent. He steps into the arena when others calculate risk from the safety of the stands. His courage isn't the absence of fear, it's the refusal to let fear have authority over his obedience.

A man who silences doubt is effective for God's purposes. He doesn't waste energy constantly questioning whether he's called; he spends that energy actually walking in the calling. He doesn't second-guess every decision to the point of paralysis; he acts on what he knows and trusts God with what he doesn't. His effectiveness comes from settled identity, not superior circumstances.

A man who rejects comparison is free to run his race with full attention. He celebrates others' victories without feeling diminished. He stays in his lane without constantly glancing at the runners beside him. His peace comes from knowing he's doing what God assigned him, regardless of what God has assigned anyone else.

This is the man the enemy fears. This is the man the world respects without quite understanding why. This is the man God can trust with influence, because influence in his hands won't be distorted by fear-based decisions, undermined by doubt-driven hesitation, or wasted on comparison-fueled competition.

The arena isn't kind to fragile men. It requires men who have fought these internal giants and developed the muscles to keep fighting them. The battles never stop, but the man who has learned to win them develops a stability that sustains him through whatever external challenges arise.

* * *

I still battle fear, doubt, and comparison. They haven't left me alone just because I've learned to fight them. But they no longer rule. They no longer get the final vote on my obedience. They no longer keep me frozen at my desk for three hours when opportunity calls.

The fight against these three is the fight that unlocks the rest of your life. As long as fear can freeze you, doubt can weaken you, and comparison can distract you, the enemy has leverage. But once you learn to move despite fear, trust despite doubt, and focus despite comparison, the rest of the battles feel smaller. You've defeated the enemies that had the most direct access to your soul.

So here's the question I want you to sit with:

Which of these three enemies is loudest in your life right now, and what would obedience look like if you refused to listen?

Is it fear, predicting disasters that haven't happened and may never happen? Is it doubt, questioning whether God really called you to what you sense He's called you to? Is it comparison, measuring your race against someone else's and finding yourself lacking?

Name it. Bring it into the light. Speak it to a brother who can remind you of truth. And then do the thing the enemy doesn't want you to do:

move anyway.

Fear, doubt, and comparison have stolen enough from you. Today is the day you start taking it back.

CHAPTER SIX

The Practice of Intentional Living

"Be very careful, then, how you live, not as unwise but as wise, making the most of every opportunity, because the days are evil."

Ephesians 5:15-16

* * *

I woke up one morning and realized I couldn't account for the previous two years. Not that I'd been unconscious, I'd been busy. Meetings filled my calendar.

Projects consumed my attention. Emails demanded responses. The days blurred into weeks, the weeks into months, the months into a stretch of time that had simply evaporated while I was looking elsewhere. I had been in constant motion, but when I tried to identify what I'd actually built, what had moved forward, what had grown, I couldn't point to much of anything of substance.

I had drifted. Not dramatically, not in ways anyone would have noticed from the outside. I still showed up. I still performed. I still hit enough targets to appear productive. But somewhere along the way, I had stopped deciding where my life was going and started letting circumstances decide for me. I had traded intentionality for reactivity, and the trade had cost me more than I realized until that morning when I sat with my coffee and genuinely couldn't remember why I'd spent the previous twenty-four months the way I had.

The worst part wasn't the time lost, though that was painful enough. The worst part was that I had been so busy being busy that I never noticed the drift happening. I hadn't made a conscious decision to coast through two years of my life. I had simply stopped making conscious decisions at all. And in the absence of intentionality, drift had filled the vacuum.

That morning became a turning point. I didn't have some dramatic revelation or mystical experience. I just saw clearly what I had allowed to happen and decided it wouldn't continue. I pulled out a notebook and started writing: Who do I want to be? What am I actually called to? What would my life look like if I lived on purpose instead of on autopilot? The answers didn't come immediately, it took months to rebuild clarity from the fog, but the process of asking was itself the beginning of living differently.

I've since learned that my story is unremarkable. Most men drift. A few live on purpose. The difference between them isn't talent, intelligence, or even opportunity. The difference is intentionality, the discipline of deciding who you want to become and building your life around that decision. It's choosing direction instead of default, alignment instead of impulse, obedience instead of convenience.

Nothing great happens by accident. And nothing God-sized happens without intention.

The Subtle Danger of Drift

Drift is the enemy of destiny, and its danger lies in its subtlety. Drift doesn't feel dangerous while it's happening. There's no alarm that sounds, no obvious warning sign, no moment where you consciously choose to abandon your calling. You just stop paying attention.

You stop checking your habits to see if they're still serving your purpose. You stop guarding your thoughts against the patterns that pull you off course. You stop challenging your excuses when they multiply. You stop fighting for the clarity that tells you where you're going and why. And slowly, silently, politely, drift takes over.

Then months go by. Sometimes years. And you wake up living a life you never consciously chose, surrounded by circumstances you never intentionally created, having become a man you never decided to become. Drift doesn't break you overnight with a dramatic collapse. It breaks you slowly, one unexamined day at a time, until the accumulated small surrenders have produced a life that bears little resemblance to your calling.

The writer of Hebrews understood this danger:

"We must pay the most careful attention, therefore, to what we have heard, so that we do not drift away." (Hebrews 2:1)

Notice the remedy: careful attention. Drift happens in the absence of attention. It fills the space left when you stop actively directing your life. The prevention is not a one-time decision but an ongoing discipline of paying attention, to your habits, your time, your relationships, your growth, your alignment with what God has called you to.

Why is drift so attractive? Because it requires nothing of you. Intentionality demands decisions, discipline, and the discomfort of saying no to good things so you can say yes to the best things. Drift demands nothing. It just lets you coast on whatever momentum already exists, responding to whatever demands feel most urgent, becoming whatever your environment shapes you into. Drift is the path of least resistance, and the path of least resistance leads away from your calling, not toward it.

Intentionality stops the drift before it steals your future. It's the discipline of staying awake to your own life, of continuously asking whether the path you're walking is the path you've chosen, or just the path you've defaulted to.

Beginning with Honest Awareness

You cannot be intentional about a life you haven't honestly assessed. Intentionality requires awareness, clear-eyed recognition of where you actually are, not where you wish you were or where you tell others you are.

This connects directly to what we explored in earlier chapters. The identity work from Chapter Two asked you to examine who you've become versus who you've presented. The fight within from Chapter Three required recognizing the internal battles you're actually facing. Confession from Chapter Four demanded speaking the truth about what you've hidden. Awareness is the common thread: you cannot change what you refuse to see.

Honest awareness means asking hard questions and sitting with the answers rather than rushing past them. Where are you wasting time, not the time you've publicly acknowledged as wasted, but the hours that disappear into scrolling, distraction, and avoidance that you've never talked about? Where are you avoiding responsibility, not dramatically, but in the small ways you set things aside, putting off hard conversations, or hope problems solve themselves? Where are you compromising your stated values, leaving a gap between what you claim matters and how you actually spend your days?

Where are you living on autopilot, going through motions without ever asking whether the motions are taking you somewhere worth going? And where do you sense the Holy Spirit nudging you toward growth that you've been resisting because it would require change you're not sure you want to make?

If you skip awareness, you skip transformation. You cannot build an intentional life on a foundation of self-deception. The structures you create will be built around a false picture of yourself, and eventually, reality will expose the gap. Leaders who can't tell themselves the truth will always sabotage their own potential, because they're building plans for a man who doesn't exist.

Awareness isn't self-condemnation. It's not beating yourself up for every failure or dwelling in shame about where you've drifted. It's simply seeing clearly, accepting the truth about your current location so you can chart a course from where you actually are rather than from where you pretend to be. A GPS is useless if you lie to it about your starting point. So is any attempt at intentional living.

Deciding Who You Will Become

Intentional living begins with a picture, not a vague aspiration but a concrete vision of the man you're choosing to become. Not the man you imagine in fantasy, but the man you're willing to build in reality, one decision at a time.

This is identity work made practical. Chapter Two established that identity comes before strategy, that who you are determines what you can build. Now we're asking: who are you actively deciding to become? Not who you hope circumstances will shape you into, but who you're deliberately constructing through your choices.

Think concretely about this man. He is disciplined, not because discipline comes naturally, but because he has built habits that hold when motivation fades. He is faithful, to his God, his wife, his commitments, his calling, even when faithfulness costs him. He is consistent, the same man in private as in public, reliable in a world that has come to expect inconsistency from leaders. He is wise, not merely intelligent, but capable of applying knowledge in ways that honor God and serve others. He is grounded, rooted in an identity that doesn't shift with circumstances or opinions.

Once you have this picture clearly in mind, every decision becomes simpler. You stop asking, "Do I feel like doing this?" Feelings are unreliable guides that shift with mood, fatigue, and circumstance. You start asking, "Does this align with who I'm becoming?" That question has a more stable answer because it's rooted in vision rather than emotion.

Paul describes this future-oriented approach to living:

"Do you not know that in a race all the runners run, but only one gets the prize? Run in such a way as to get the prize. Everyone who competes in the games goes into strict training. They do it to get a crown that will not last, but we do it to get a crown that will last forever."
(1 Corinthians 9:24-25)

Athletes train intentionally. They don't stumble into Olympic conditioning, they decide what they want to achieve and then structure their lives around achieving it. They say no to countless things that would pull them off course. They endure discomfort today for victory tomorrow. Paul says believers should approach life with the same intentionality, but for stakes far higher than any earthly prize.

Identity leads; intentionality follows. When you know who you're becoming, you know what to build. When you know what to build, you know what to do today. The vision creates the framework; the framework guides the decisions; the decisions shape the man.

The Freedom of Structure

You cannot live intentionally in a chaotic system. Without structure, every decision becomes a fresh negotiation between your intentions and your impulses, and impulses win more often than most men want to admit. Structure is the framework that protects your intentionality when willpower runs low.

This runs counter to how many men think about structure. They see it as restriction, as the enemy of freedom and spontaneity. But the opposite is true. Structure doesn't trap you, it frees you. It frees you from the exhaustion of constantly deciding what to do. It frees you from the tyranny of whatever feels urgent in the moment. It frees you from the drift that consumes unstructured time.

Structure is the container that allows intentionality to survive contact with daily life.

What does structure look like in practice? It looks like rhythms that repeat regardless of how you feel, morning routines that orient your day, weekly patterns that ensure important things don't get lost, regular reviews that assess whether you're still on course. It looks like habits that have become so automatic they don't require decision-making energy anymore, you don't have to decide whether to pray, read Scripture, exercise, or invest in your marriage; you've built systems that make these things happen as reliably as brushing your teeth.

Consider what an intentional morning might look like. Before the demands of the day begin their assault, you've already spent time with God, not because you felt particularly spiritual, but because that's what this time of day is for. You've oriented your mind toward truth, reviewed your priorities, and prepared yourself for the battles ahead. By the time the first email arrives or the first meeting starts, you're operating from a foundation you've deliberately laid rather than scrambling to find your footing.

Consider what an intentional week might include. A protected time for the deep work that matters most, scheduled before less important demands can crowd it out. A regular conversation with your spouse that ensures your marriage doesn't drift while you're busy elsewhere. A rhythm of exercise that keeps your body capable of the work God calls you to. A meeting with brothers who know your struggles and hold you accountable. A Sabbath rest that acknowledges you're not the one holding the universe together.

Spiritual maturity thrives under structure. Immaturity hates structure because structure kills excuses. When you've built a system that makes the right things happen, , you can no longer claim you didn't have time, forgot, or couldn't fit it in. The structure reveals your true priorities by making clear what you're willing to protect and what you're willing to sacrifice.

The Truth Your Calendar Tells

Your calendar reveals your real priorities, not the priorities you claim, but the priorities you actually live. This is uncomfortable but essential to recognize.

You can say God comes first, but if your calendar shows no protected time for prayer, Scripture, and spiritual formation, you're living a different story than you're telling. You can say your health matters, but if weeks pass without scheduled exercise, you're prioritizing something else. You can say you value your marriage, but if date nights and meaningful conversations only happen when nothing else demands attention, your calendar is telling the truth about where your spouse actually ranks.

Intentional living requires intentional scheduling. Purpose must be planned, not hoped for. If something matters to you, it needs a place on your calendar, a protected slot that other things cannot easily displace. What gets scheduled gets done; what remains vague intention often remains undone.

This is why Paul urges believers to make the most of their time:

"Be very careful, then, how you live, not as unwise but as wise, making the most of every opportunity, because the days are evil." (Ephesians 5:15-16)

The phrase translated "making the most of every opportunity" literally means "redeeming the time" buying back time from the waste that would otherwise claim it. Time is constantly being spent; the question is whether you're spending it intentionally or letting it drain away. The wise person lives carefully, aware that time is limited and valuable and easily lost.

Auditing your calendar periodically is a practice of honest awareness applied to time. Look at the last month: Where did your hours actually go? What got protected, and what got sacrificed when conflicts arose? What important things never happened because they never got scheduled? This audit often reveals gaps between stated values and lived priorities, gaps that can only be closed through intentional rescheduling, not better intentions.

Your time has to match your values. If it doesn't, you're living a lie without realizing it, telling a story about your priorities that your actual life contradicts every day.

The Discipline of No

Intentional living is as much about what you refuse as what you pursue. Every yes costs you something: time, energy, focus, peace. You cannot say yes to everything and live intentionally, the math doesn't work. If you don't choose what to say no to, circumstances will choose for you, and they won't choose wisely.

Leaders who say yes to everything end up drained, scattered, and ineffective. They're so busy doing many things that they never do anything well. They exhaust themselves responding to demands without ever advancing toward their calling.

Their calendar fills with other people's priorities while their own purposes remain neglected.

Jesus modeled selective engagement throughout His ministry. He withdrew from crowds that wanted more from Him. He prioritized the twelve over the masses, and the three over the twelve. He refused to be controlled by urgent demands when Father-given priorities pointed elsewhere. His no to some things enabled His yes to the things that mattered most.

You must learn to say no to distractions that masquerade as opportunities. Not everything that presents itself deserves your attention. Not every open door is meant to be walked through. Not every good thing is your thing. The enemy doesn't need to destroy you with obviously harmful pursuits; he can derail your calling just as effectively by filling your life with good things that aren't your things, diluting your focus until you have no concentrated impact anywhere.

You must say no to draining people who consume your energy without reciprocating investment. This doesn't mean abandoning everyone who's struggling, serving others is central to following Jesus. But it means recognizing when someone has become a drain rather than a relationship, when their demands are endless rather than seasonal, when your engagement with them is preventing you from fulfilling your responsibilities to others.

You must say no to anything that pulls you out of alignment with who you're becoming. When an opportunity arises, the question isn't only "Is this good?" The question is "Does this fit?" Does it align with my calling? Does it serve my mission? Does it move me toward the man I'm becoming, or does it pull me sideways into someone else's vision?

Saying no doesn't make you harsh, unhelpful, or unchristian. It makes you faithful, faithful to what God has assigned you, faithful to the people who depend on your focused presence, faithful to the future He's building in you. A scattered yes to everything is less loving than a focused yes to the right things.

Spirit-Led Intentionality

Everything we've discussed could be practiced by anyone, regardless of faith. Structure, discipline, time management, selective engagement, these are principles that work for men generally. But intentional living divorced from God becomes self-help, and self-help runs out of fuel quickly.

Spirit-led intentionality is fundamentally different. In this framework, God gives the direction, you're not inventing your purpose; you're discovering what He's already designed. God gives the wisdom, you're not figuring out the path alone; you're receiving guidance from the One who sees the whole picture. God gives the conviction, the internal prompting that tells you when you're drifting and calls you back. God gives the strength, the power to do what your willpower alone could never sustain.

You give the obedience. That's your part. God supplies everything else, but He will not obey for you. He provides direction, but you have to walk. He provides strength, but you have to apply it. He provides correction, but you have to receive it and adjust.

This is why intentional living works only when your will aligns with God's will.

You can structure your life beautifully around purposes that aren't His purposes, and you'll build something that may look impressive but lacks eternal significance. True intentionality starts with surrender: "Not my will, but Yours."

From that starting point, you build a life aligned with what God is actually doing, not what you've independently decided sounds good.

"Commit to the Lord whatever you do, and he will establish your plans." Proverbs 16:3

Notice the sequence: commitment comes first. You bring your plans, your intentions, your structures to God and surrender them to His purposes. Then He establishes them, gives them stability, success, and meaning they wouldn't have on their own. Uncommitted plans lack this foundation. They may be impressive, but they're not established by God.

This produces an alignment that creates power and clarity no human system can manufacture. When you're walking in sync with what God is doing, when your intentionality serves His purposes rather than just your ambitions, there's a rightness that sustains you through difficulty. You're not grinding through life on willpower; you're flowing with something larger than yourself.

When Structure Collapses

Life disrupts even the best structures. Crisis arrives. Transitions upend familiar rhythms. Circumstances beyond your control demolish the systems you've carefully built. What then?

The temptation in these seasons is to abandon intentionality entirely, to use the disruption as an excuse for drift. "Things are too crazy right now to maintain my rhythms." "I'll get back to intentional living once things settle down." But this is often exactly backwards. The seasons when structure collapses are the seasons when intentionality matters most. Without external structure holding you together, internal resolve becomes even more essential.

When your normal rhythms are impossible, you don't abandon intentionality, you adapt it. Maybe your morning routine that worked beautifully now runs into impossible demands. Find a different time. Maybe the weekly rhythm that protected important things can't be maintained. Rebuild it around whatever remains possible. The specific structures may change; the commitment to living on purpose rather than drifting doesn't.

Jesus offers wisdom for seasons when external circumstances are beyond control:

"Therefore do not worry about tomorrow, for tomorrow will worry about itself. Each day has enough trouble of its own."
Matthew 6:34

In chaotic seasons, intentionality sometimes shrinks to a single day or even a single moment. You can't plan a month ahead because you don't know what next week holds. Fine. Be intentional today. Be intentional this hour. Ask: What does obedience look like right now? What does alignment require in this moment?

Intentionality scales to whatever time horizon you can actually see.

Difficult seasons also reveal which of your structures were essential and which were optional. When everything gets stripped away, you discover what you truly cannot live without, the non-negotiable rhythms that keep you anchored to God and to purpose. Everything else can be rebuilt when stability returns. But those core rhythms become the framework around which everything else is constructed.

Brotherhood matters especially in these seasons. The accountability and encouragement of men who know your struggles can hold you to intentionality when your own resolve wavers. They can remind you of who you're becoming when circumstances have made you forget. They can pray for you when you lack the strength to pray for yourself. The community you built in stable times becomes the lifeline that sustains you in unstable ones.

What Intentional Living Produces

A man who learns to live intentionally becomes something the world doesn't expect and the enemy doesn't want.

He develops confidence, not the fragile confidence that comes from external validation, but the stable confidence that comes from alignment. When your actions match your values, when your habits match your identity, when your days reflect your calling, confidence grows naturally. You're not pretending to be someone you're not; you're actually becoming the man you've decided to become. That congruence produces a settledness that can't be manufactured.

He becomes focused in a world of distraction. While others scatter their attention across dozens of demands without impact in any, the intentional man concentrates his energy where it matters most. He accomplishes more with less frantic activity because he's not wasting effort on things that don't align with his calling. His focus makes him effective where scattered men are merely busy.

He becomes steady in a world of reactivity. While others lurch from urgency to urgency, controlled by whatever screams loudest, the intentional man operates from a center that doesn't shift. He can respond to genuine emergencies without being hijacked by manufactured ones. His stability makes him trustworthy when unstable men are unpredictable.

The world expects men to be distracted, fragile, addicted to immediate gratification, and unsure of their purpose. A man who knows who he is, where he's going, what matters most, and how to align his days around those truths is a threat to every pattern of darkness that depends on disoriented men. He's dangerous because he lives on purpose, and purpose is exactly what the enemy wants to steal.

The arena consumes distracted men, men who drift in without clarity or preparation get overwhelmed by battles they never saw coming. But the arena elevates intentional men, men who enter knowing who they are, what they're fighting for, and how to sustain themselves through the long battles ahead. You can't drift your way into influence. You can't stumble your way into calling. You can't half-commit your way into a life that honors God. Intentionality is required.

* * *

That morning when I realized I couldn't account for two years of my life was painful. But the pain became the catalyst for rebuilding everything around intentionality rather than drift. The structures I've developed since then aren't perfect, they've been disrupted and rebuilt multiple times. But the commitment to living on purpose has remained, and that commitment has changed the trajectory of everything.

Intentional living is the practical application of everything this book has been building toward. Your identity from Chapter Two provides the vision. The fight within from Chapter Three is engaged daily through intentional discipline. Confession and conviction from Chapter Four become built-in rhythms rather than crisis responses. Fear, doubt, and comparison from Chapter Five are confronted through structures that don't give them space to grow.

So here's the question I want you to sit with:

Where has drift crept into your life, and what one structure could you build this week to stop it?

Not a complete overhaul of everything, that's overwhelming and usually unsustainable. One structure. One rhythm. One protected time for something that matters. Maybe it's a morning routine that orients your day. Maybe it's a weekly conversation that's been neglected. Maybe it's Sabbath rest you've been stealing from yourself. Maybe it's time with a brother who can hold you accountable.

Start there. Build one intentional structure this week. Let it become the foundation for the next one. The life you're meant to live is built one decision at a time, one rhythm at a time, one day at a time.

The arena is waiting for men who refuse to drift. The question is whether you'll be one of them.

CHAPTER SEVEN

The Importance of Daily Habits

"Whoever can be trusted with very little can also be trusted with much, and whoever is dishonest with very little will also be dishonest with much."

Luke 16:10

* * *

The habit that changed my life took less than fifteen minutes a day.

I had tried dramatic overhauls before, complete life restructurings that collapsed within weeks. I had made grand commitments on New Year's mornings that were forgotten by February. I had read books about transformation and felt inspired, only to find myself unchanged three months later. The pattern was so consistent that I had started to believe real change simply wasn't available to someone with my particular weaknesses.

Then a mentor gave me advice that seemed almost insultingly simple: "Stop trying to change your life. Just change your morning."

He suggested I wake up fifteen minutes earlier, just fifteen minutes, and spend that time in Scripture and prayer before anything else. Not an hour of deep study. Not an elaborate spiritual discipline. Just fifteen minutes of reading and talking to God before the day began its assault. "You can do anything for fifteen minutes," he said. "Start there."

I was skeptical. Fifteen minutes seemed too small to matter. But everything else had failed, so I tried it. The first morning was awkward and unremarkable. So was the second. But by the end of the first week, something subtle had shifted. My days felt different, not because my circumstances had changed, but because I was entering them from a different starting point. By the end of the first month, the fifteen minutes had grown to thirty, not because I forced it but because I wanted more of what that time was producing.

Within six months, that single habit had become the anchor for others. The discipline I developed in the morning started leaking into other areas. My physical habits improved. My mental diet changed. My emotional responses became more measured. One small habit, repeated daily, had catalyzed a transformation that years of dramatic gestures had failed to produce.

I've since learned that this is how change actually works. Not through inspiration but through repetition. Not through grand intentions but through small actions, repeated until they become who you are. Your life is made of your habits, not your dreams, not your intentions, not your potential. Your habits. And the distance between the life you're living and the life you're called to live is almost always a gap in habits, not a gap in desire.

The Truth Your Habits Tell

You can talk about priorities all day. You can declare that God comes first, that your health matters, that your family is your highest earthly priority, that your calling deserves your best energy. But your habits tell the truth about what you actually value, not what you claim to value, but what you've proven you value through repeated action.

This is uncomfortable but essential to recognize. A man who says he values Scripture but hasn't opened his Bible in weeks is telling a different story than he thinks. A man who says health matters but hasn't exercised in months is living a contradiction. A man who claims his marriage is a priority but spends every evening on his phone instead of with his wife is deceiving himself about his actual values.

Habits expose reality; words can obscure it.

This is why Jesus taught that faithfulness in small things reveals capacity for larger things:

"Whoever can be trusted with very little can also be trusted with much, and whoever is dishonest with very little will also be dishonest with much." Luke 16:10

The "very little" in your life is your daily habits, the small, repeated actions that no one notices and no one applauds. These habits reveal your trustworthiness more accurately than any major decision because they show what you do when nothing's at stake, when no one's watching, when there's no immediate consequence for choosing the easier path. God uses these small tests to determine readiness for larger assignments. The man who cannot be faithful in the little thing of a morning habit cannot be trusted with the large thing of significant influence.

A man is not shaped by his intentions. He is shaped by what he repeats. This is why people with enormous potential often accomplish little, their intentions were grand, but their habits were weak. And it's why people with modest natural talent sometimes accomplish extraordinary things, their habits were strong enough to compound their abilities over time. Habits are the great equalizer, turning potential into reality or leaving it unrealized.

How Habits Build Identity

Chapter Two established that identity comes before strategy, that who you are determines what you can build. Now we need to understand how identity is actually formed. It doesn't come from inspiration. It doesn't come from information. It comes from repetition.

You don't become disciplined because you feel disciplined. Feelings follow action, not the other way around. You become disciplined because you act disciplined, because you do the disciplined thing when you don't feel like it, and then do it again, and again, until the action has reshaped your sense of who you are. Every time you keep a commitment you made to yourself, you're casting a vote for the identity of someone who keeps commitments. Accumulate enough votes, and that becomes who you are.

This is why habits build identity faster than inspiration ever could. Inspiration gives you a feeling; habits give you evidence. When you've maintained a habit for months, you have proof that you're the kind of person who maintains that habit. The identity isn't theoretical, it's demonstrated. You're not hoping to become disciplined; you're looking at a track record that proves you already are.

James understood the relationship between action and identity:

> *"Do not merely listen to the word, and so deceive yourselves. Do what it says."*
> *James 1:22*

Notice the warning: merely listening leads to self-deception. You can hear truth, feel inspired by truth, even agree wholeheartedly with truth, and still deceive yourself about who you are if you don't actually do anything with it. The doing is what matters. The repeated doing is what builds the identity. Without action, you're not being transformed; you're just being informed, and information without implementation is self-deception.

This means you don't need more inspiration, you probably have enough inspiration stored up from books, sermons, and conversations to last a lifetime. You need more repetition. You need to take what you already know and do it so consistently that it becomes who you are. Every time you choose self-control, obedience, discipline, or faithfulness, you're reinforcing the identity you're building. Every time you choose the opposite, you're reinforcing that identity instead. There is no neutral ground. Every repeated action is shaping who you're becoming.

The Power of Faithful Smallness

The world tells you to think big, massive goals, audacious visions, world-changing ambitions. There's a place for that. But Scripture offers a different emphasis: be faithful in little.

Big goals without daily habits are fantasies. You can envision an incredible future all you want, but if your daily actions don't move you toward it, the vision is just pleasant imagination. The goal doesn't do the work, the habits do. And a man without aligned habits is a man whose goals will remain permanently out of reach, always inspiring, never achieved.

Conversely, small habits without big goals still create progress. A man who doesn't have a grand vision but who faithfully practices good habits will end up somewhere meaningful, carried forward by the compound effect of consistent action. He may not have planned his destination, but his habits will deliver him somewhere better than where he started.

The Israelites learned this lesson in the wilderness through manna:

"Each morning everyone gathered as much as they needed, and when the sun grew hot, it melted away... No one is to keep any of it until morning." Exodus 16:21-19

God provided exactly what they needed for each day, no more. They couldn't stockpile for the week. They couldn't gather once and coast on what they'd collected. Every morning required fresh gathering. This was God training His people in the discipline of daily faithfulness, teaching them that provision comes through consistent daily action, not occasional massive effort.

This is how habits work. You cannot stockpile discipline. You cannot do a week's worth of prayer on Sunday and coast until next weekend. You cannot exercise intensely once a month and expect the benefits of daily movement. The gathering must be daily. The faithfulness must be consistent. The habit must be repeated to produce its compounding effect.

Big goals collapse under inconsistent habits, while small habits compound into results far greater than the daily effort seems to warrant. This is the mathematics of faithfulness: tiny investments, made consistently over time, produce returns that dwarf any single dramatic gesture.

Understanding How Habits Actually Work

If habits are so important, why are they so hard to build? Understanding the mechanics of habit formation helps you work with your nature rather than against it.

Every habit operates through a loop: a cue that triggers the behavior, the routine itself, and a reward that reinforces it. This loop explains both why bad habits are hard to break and why good habits can be built. When you understand thecue-routine-reward pattern, you can engineer new habits rather than just hoping they'll develop.

Consider how this works with a habit like morning Scripture reading. The cue might be your alarm going off or your coffee finishing brewing. The routine is the reading itself. The reward is both the immediate sense of starting your day grounded and the cumulative sense of becoming someone who reads Scripture daily. Stack the right cue with the right routine and reward, and the habit becomes increasingly automatic.

Environment matters enormously. Your physical environment is constantly cueing behaviors, either the ones you want or the ones you're trying to escape. If your phone is next to your bed, it's cuing the habit of checking it first thing in the morning. If your Bible is on your nightstand instead, it's cuing a different first action. Much of habit change isn't about willpower; it's about designing an environment that cues the behaviors you want and removes cues for the behaviors you don't.

Starting small matters more than starting ambitious. My mentor was right: fifteen minutes was achievable when an hour would have failed. When you make a habit small enough that it requires minimal willpower, you remove the resistance that kills most habits in their infancy. You can always expand a habit once it's established. You cannot establish a habit that's so large it overwhelms your capacity from day one.

Habit stacking accelerates formation. Attaching a new habit to an existing one borrows the established habit's strength. "After I pour my morning coffee, I will read Scripture for ten minutes" is more likely to succeed than a vague intention to read Scripture sometime during the day. The existing habit becomes the cue for the new one, and you're building on foundation rather than starting from nothing.

Identity-based habits prove most durable. When you frame a habit as evidence of who you are rather than just something you do, it becomes self-reinforcing. "I'm the kind of man who reads Scripture every morning" is more powerful than "I'm trying to read Scripture more." The first is an identity statement that every completed reading reinforces. The second is a vague aspiration that can be abandoned without contradiction.

The Habits That Build a Man

Habits operate across every domain of your life. Neglecting any domain creates weakness that eventually affects the others. A holistic approach to habit-building recognizes that spiritual, physical, mental, and emotional habits are interconnected, each supporting and reinforcing the others.

Spiritual habits anchor everything else. Without them, your life becomes entirely reactive, driven by circumstances rather than rooted in truth. Scripture reading gives you daily access to God's voice and perspective. Prayer connects you to the Source of strength you'll need throughout the day. Silence creates space to hear what constant noise drowns out. Confession keeps your accounts short with God and others. Sabbath rest reminds you that you're not the one holding the universe together. These aren't religious chores to check off; they're spiritual weapons that align your heart, sharpen your mind, and strengthen your spirit. Spiritual habits create spiritual authority, the kind that can't be manufactured but must be cultivated through consistent practice.

Physical habits affect your capacity for everything else. Your body is not separate from your calling; it's the vehicle through which you fulfill it. If your body is weak, tired, or undisciplined, it affects your leadership, your mental clarity, your emotional stability, and even your spiritual receptivity. Movement keeps your body capable of the work ahead. Sleep restores what each day depletes. Nutrition fuels the engine that everything else depends on. Physical habits aren't vanity, they're stewardship. You cannot lead well when you're physically collapsing. You fight better when your body works with you rather than against you.

Mental habits determine where your focus goes, and where your focus goes, your life follows. What you consume, what you read, watch, listen to, scroll through, shapes how you think. Some men lose the internal fight not because they lack spiritual desire but because they feed their minds garbage and then wonder why clarity eludes them. Guarding your mental inputs isn't prudishness; it's strategic warfare. Your mind is the battlefield from Chapter Three, and your mental habits determine whether you're strengthening or weakening your position.

Emotional habits shape your stability over time. The way you respond to anger, frustration, disappointment, or stress may feel automatic, but those responses are habits, patterns you've practiced until they became reflexive. If you react explosively, withdraw defensively, spiral anxiously, or avoid compulsively, you've trained those responses through repetition. But emotional maturity is built the same way: one intentional response at a time, practiced until it becomes your new default. A steady man isn't born steady, he becomes steady by practicing steadiness when unsteadiness would be easier.

When You Fall Off

Every man who builds habits also fails at habits. The question isn't whether you'll miss a day or break a streak, you will. The question is what you do afterward.

The enemy's strategy after a habit failure is predictable: shame, then abandonment. He wants you to feel so bad about missing once that you give up entirely. "See? You can't do this. Why bother trying?" This is the voice that has derailed countless habit attempts, not the initial failure, but the shame spiral that follows it, convincing you that one miss proves permanent incapacity.

But one miss doesn't break a habit. Missing twice in a row starts to. The goal after any failure is simple: never miss twice. Miss once, and you're still building. Miss twice, and the old pattern starts reasserting itself. Get back to the habit as quickly as possible, without elaborate self-flagellation, without demanding extra performance to make up for the miss, without turning a single failure into evidence of permanent defeat.

This is where confession and correction from Chapter Four becomes practical.

When you fail at a habit, confess it, to God and, if the habit is one you've shared with a brother, to him as well. Then correct: identify what went wrong and adjust. Then continue: return to the habit without extended self-punishment. Confess, correct, continue. The same rhythm that works for moral failure works for habit failure.

Sometimes habits fail because they are too ambitious. If you're failing repeatedly at a habit, the answer might not be more willpower but a smaller habit. Reduce the scope until it's achievable, establish consistency at that level, then expand. There's no shame in making a habit easier, there's wisdom in it. The point is not impressive-looking habits; the point is habits that actually hold.

Sometimes habits fail because life genuinely disrupted them. Illness, crisis, travel, major transitions, these can destroy established rhythms. When stability returns, you rebuild. You've built the habit before; you can build it again. The neural pathways are still there. The identity you developed hasn't disappeared. Getting back to a broken habit is easier than building it the first time, as long as you don't let shame keep you away.

The Power of Brotherhood in Habits

Throughout this book, we've established that the fight within isn't meant to be fought alone. This applies directly to habit formation. Habits built in isolation are more fragile than habits built in community.

Accountability dramatically increases habit success rates. When someone else knows what you're building and checks in on your progress, you have an external reinforcement that your own willpower lacks. You'll get up for the workout you'd skip if no one knew about it. You'll complete the reading you'd postpone if no one was asking. The knowledge that someone will inquire adds weight to the commitment in a way that purely private resolutions don't have.

But accountability is more than surveillance. A brother who knows your habit-building goals can encourage you when motivation fades, celebrate with you when milestones pass, help you troubleshoot when patterns aren't working, and remind you of who you're becoming when failure makes you forget. This isrelationship in service of transformation, exactly what the body of Christ is designed to provide.

Consider sharing your habit-building with at least one trusted brother. Tell him what you're trying to build and why. Give him permission to ask you about it. Invite his encouragement and, when needed, his correction. This isn't weakness; it's wisdom. The man who tries to build habits entirely alone is rejecting the help God offers through community.

"Two are better than one, because they have a good return for their labor: If either of them falls down, one can help the other up. But pity anyone who falls and has no one to help them up." Ecclesiastes 4:9-10

The imagery is of physical assistance when someone stumbles, exactly what's needed in habit formation. You will fall down. You will fail. The question is whether you have someone to help you back up or whether you're lying alone, with no one to extend a hand. Build your habits within community, and you have a support system for the inevitable failures. Build them alone, and you have only yourself to lift you, and that's often not enough.

You Fall to Your Habits

There's a common saying that people rise to the occasion when pressure comes. It sounds encouraging. It's also largely false.

The truth is that you don't rise to the occasion, you fall to your habits. Under pressure, you don't suddenly become a better man. You become the man your habits have trained you to be. Stress strips away pretense and exposes the patterns you've actually built. Crisis reveals character, but the character it reveals was formed long before the crisis arrived, through thousands of small decisions that felt inconsequential at the time.

This is why building strong habits during calm seasons matters so much.

You're not just making your ordinary days better; you're preparing for the days that won't be ordinary. The discipline you develop when nothing's at stake becomes the strength you draw on when everything is. The self-control you practice inlow-pressure situations becomes available in high-pressure ones, but only if you've actually practiced it.

Paul used athletic training as an analogy for exactly this reason:

"Everyone who competes in the games goes into strict training. They do it to get a crown that will not last, but we do it to get a crown that will last forever. Therefore I do not run like someone running aimlessly; I do not fight like a boxer beating the air."
1 Corinthians 9:25-26

Athletes don't perform well by accident. They perform well because they've trained well, hours, days, months, years of disciplined preparation for the moments of competition. When the race begins, they rely on what training has built into their bodies and minds. They don't have time to think through every movement; they fall back on habits that have become automatic through repetition.

Your daily habits are your training. The arena is your competition. When pressure hits, when crisis arrives, when temptation strikes at a vulnerable moment, when stress pushes you toward your worst tendencies, you will respond with whatever patterns your training has established. If you've built habits of prayer, you'll pray. If you've built habits of truth-telling, you'll tell truth. If you've built habits of self-control, you'll access self-control. But if you haven't built these habits, they won't magically appear when you need them most.

Pressure becomes a platform for the man with strong habits, a chance to demonstrate what he's built. But pressure becomes a threat to the man with weak habits, an exposure of what he's failed to develop. Same pressure, different outcomes, determined entirely by the training that preceded the moment.

Habits That Outlive You

Your habits don't just shape your days. They shape your legacy.

The habits you build today become the inheritance you leave behind. Your children watch what you do far more than they hear what you say, and what they watch becomes the template for what they build in their own lives. A father with consistent habits of Scripture reading, prayer, and spiritual discipline is training his children in those patterns whether he explicitly teaches them or not. A father with consistent habits of anger, avoidance, and self-indulgence is training his children in those patterns too.

This is both the weight and the gift of habit-building. The weight is that you're not just shaping yourself, you're shaping everyone watching. The gift is that by building strong habits, you're giving a legacy that requires no speech, no special moment, no dramatic gesture. You're just living a life that demonstrates what faithfulness looks like, and that demonstration teaches more than any lecture ever could.

Your future family benefits from the habits you build today. Your community follows the patterns you establish. Your influence multiplies because your character was consistent. Legacy isn't primarily about what you leave people; it's about who you were while you were with them. And who you were is formed by what you did repeatedly, your habits.

When you build strong habits, legacy becomes almost unavoidable. You don't have to plan an elaborate inheritance; you just have to live with enough consistency that the watching world, starting with your own family, absorbs what you've modeled. The faithful man doesn't need to strategize his legacy. He just needs to keep showing up, day after day, and let the compound effect of faithful habits speak for itself.

* * *

That fifteen-minute morning habit from years ago is still with me, grown and adapted, but still the foundation that holds everything else. It taught me that transformation doesn't require massive changes. It requires small changes, made consistently, until they become who you are.

The arena doesn't reward potential. It doesn't care how talented you are or how big your dreams might be. The arena rewards consistency, the daily faithfulness that turns intention into reality, one habit at a time. The man with strong habits is grounded when others are scattered, steady when others are reactive, prepared when others are scrambling. That man is dangerous, not because he's more gifted, but because he's more disciplined. And discipline, repeated daily, produces results that natural talent alone never can.

So here's the question I want you to sit with:

What one habit, kept faithfully for the next ninety days, would most change the trajectory of your life?

Not five habits. Not a complete life overhaul. One habit. Small enough to be achievable, significant enough to matter, consistent enough to compound. Maybe it's the morning Scripture time that anchors everything else. Maybe it's the exercise that your body has been begging for. Maybe it's the weekly conversation with your wife that your marriage needs. Maybe it's the time with a brother who can hold you accountable.

Choose one. Start this week. Make it small enough to succeed. Tell someone who will ask you about it. And then show up, day after day, until the habit becomes who you are.

Your life is made of your habits. Build them well, and everything else follows.

CHAPTER EIGHT

Accountability as Ownership

"From everyone who has been given much, much will be demanded; and from the one who has been entrusted with much, much more will be asked."

Luke 12:48

* * *

I had been avoiding him for three weeks.

We had agreed to meet weekly, that was the arrangement. He would ask me the hard questions about my relationships, my habits, my integrity, my walk with God. I would answer honestly. That was the deal we'd made, two men who recognized we needed someone in our lives who wouldn't let us drift.

But I had been slipping. Not in some dramatic way, just the slow erosion that happens when you stop paying attention. My morning discipline had grown inconsistent. My patience with my family had worn thin. A compromise I'd made weeks ago had started growing roots I didn't want to examine. And the last thing I wanted was to sit across from someone who would ask me directly about these things.

So I made excuses. Schedule conflicts. Last-minute emergencies. Vague unavailability that was really just avoidance dressed up as busyness. I told myself I'd reconnect with him once I got my act together, once I had something better to report than the truth of where I actually was.

He saw through it immediately. After the third week, he showed up at my house unannounced, sat down across from my desk, and said, "You're hiding. What's going on?"

I wanted to be offended. I wanted to deflect. I wanted to explain how busy I'd been, how the schedule just hadn't worked out, how it wasn't personal. But he just sat there, waiting, with the patience of a man who wasn't going to accept excuses. And in that silence, something broke in me.

I told him everything. The slipping habits. The growing tension at home. The compromise I'd been pretending wasn't serious. The shame I felt about all of it, which had been feeding my avoidance, which had been making everything worse. I laid it all out, and when I finished, I felt something I hadn't expected: relief.

He didn't lecture me. He didn't shame me. He just said, "Okay. Now we know where you are. Let's figure out what needs to happen next." And over the following weeks, with his consistent presence holding me accountable, I rebuilt what I'd let erode.

That experience taught me something I've never forgotten: accountability isn't punishment. It's ownership. It's the discipline of taking full responsibility for your actions, your choices, your habits, and your direction, and inviting others into that process because you know you can't see yourself clearly enough to do it alone.

Most men avoid accountability because it forces them to confront what they'd rather hide. Strong men pursue accountability because it keeps them sharp, catches drift early, and prevents small erosions from becoming catastrophic collapses.

Accountability isn't about guilt. It's about growth.

The Foundation of Leadership

You cannot lead others if you cannot lead yourself. And you cannot lead yourself without ownership, the willingness to take full responsibility for what's in your control without deflecting to circumstances, other people, emotional states, or convenient excuses.

Ownership is a posture toward life that says: "If it's in my life, I'm responsible for it." Not responsible for everything that happens to you, you don't control other people's choices or circumstances beyond your influence. But responsible for your response. Responsible for what you do with what you've been given. Responsible for holding the line; persevering with the habits, making the choices, and walking the path that God has placed before you.

This posture eliminates the escape routes that keep men stuck. No more excuses, the easy explanations that absolve you of responsibility while ensuring nothing changes. No more deflection, pointing to external factors so you don't have to examine internal ones. No more blame-shifting, making someone else the reason for your failure so you don't have to face your own contribution. No more victim mindset, the posture that makes you the passive recipient of life rather than an active agent in it.

Jesus told a parable about a master who entrusted his property to servants before leaving on a journey. To one he gave five talents, to another two, to another one, each according to their ability. When he returned, he held each servant accountable for what they'd done with what they'd been given. The servants who had multiplied their talents were praised and given more. The servant who had buried his talent out of fear was condemned, not for lacking ability, but for failing to steward what he'd received.

"His master replied, 'Well done, good and faithful servant! You have been faithful with a few things; I will put you in charge of many things.'" Matthew 25:21

The language here is the language of accountability: stewardship, faithfulness, responsibility, giving account. The master expected his servants to do something with what they'd been given, and he held them responsible for the results. This is how God operates. He gives gifts, opportunities, responsibilities, and then holds us accountable for what we do with them. Leadership begins the moment you stop waiting for someone else to fix what you control and start taking ownership of what you've been given.

Why We Resist What We Need

If accountability is so valuable, why do most men resist it? Understanding the resistance helps you overcome it.

The first reason is fear of exposure. Accountability shines light on the parts of your life that prefer darkness. It exposes laziness you've been excusing, denial you've been maintaining, hidden patterns you've been pretending don't exist. The prospect of having someone see these things clearly, and having to acknowledge them yourself, creates an instinctive pull toward avoidance. This was exactly what drove my three weeks of hiding: I didn't want to speak out loud what I'd been tolerating in secret.

The second reason is pride. Pride interprets accountability as attack rather than assistance. When someone asks you a hard question, pride hears criticism: "You're judging me. You're against me. You don't understand my situation." Humility hears something different: "I need this. I can grow from this. Tell me the truth." Pride protects your feelings in the moment while sabotaging your future. Humility accepts temporary discomfort for the sake of long-term growth.

The third reason is past negative experiences. Many men have encountered accountability that was harsh, controlling, or shame-based rather than loving and growth-oriented. They've been in relationships where "accountability" was really just criticism without grace, or surveillance without trust, or power dynamics disguised as spiritual care. These experiences create legitimate wariness about entering new accountability relationships, wariness that must be acknowledged rather than dismissed.

The fourth reason is the illusion of self-sufficiency. Many men believe they should be able to handle things on their own, that needing accountability is a sign of weakness rather than wisdom. This is particularly true for leaders, who often feel that admitting need would undermine their authority. But the opposite is true: the leader who refuses accountability becomes increasingly blind to his own weaknesses, while the leader who embraces it develops the self-awareness that makes him trustworthy.

Recognizing these resistance patterns in yourself is the first step to overcoming them. When you feel the pull to avoid accountability, ask: Is this the fear of exposure trying to keep me in darkness? Is this pride interpreting help as attack? Is this past pain making me wary of future good? Is this false self-sufficiency pretending I don't need what I clearly do? Naming the resistance diminishes its power.

What Accountability Actually Does

Understanding accountability's purpose helps you pursue it rather than avoid it. Accountability is not primarily about catching failure, it's about creating alignment.

God doesn't hold you accountable to shame you. He holds you accountable to strengthen you, to correct your direction when you've drifted, sharpen your character where it's grown dull, develop discipline you haven't built, protect your calling from self-sabotage, and align your life with truth. A life without accountability becomes a life without alignment, and misalignment, left uncorrected, eventually becomes destruction.

This is the message throughout Hebrews 12, where God's discipline is compared to a father's training of his children:

> *"No discipline seems pleasant at the time, but painful. Later on, however, it produces a harvest of righteousness and peace for those who have been trained by it." Hebrews 12:11*

Notice the sequence: discipline is painful in the moment but produces a harvest of righteousness and peace over time. The discomfort of accountability is an investment that pays dividends. The man who avoids accountability avoids the discomfort, but also forfeits the harvest. He stays comfortable while his life drifts further from alignment.

Accountability also creates consistency by replacing wishful thinking with measurable action. When you know someone will ask whether you followed through, you're more likely to follow through. When you know you'll have to report on your habits, your habits become more reliable. When someone is watching, not as surveillance but as support, the consistency that seemed impossible when you were alone becomes achievable.

We saw this in Chapter Seven when discussing habits. Accountability dramatically increases habit success rates because it adds external reinforcement to internal intention. But this applies beyond habits to every area of life: marriage, parenting, leadership, integrity. The presence of loving accountability makes excellence possible where isolation produced mediocrity.

The Layers of Accountability

Accountability isn't monolithic. It operates in different ways at different levels, and a man needs multiple forms of accountability working together.

The first layer is accountability to God. This is the foundational level, the recognition that you will ultimately give account to the One who sees everything, including what no human eye observes. This accountability exists whether you acknowledge it or not. The psalmist understood this: "You have searched me, Lord, and you know me. You know when I sit and when I rise; you perceive my thoughts from afar." Living in awareness of God's constant knowledge shapes how you behave when no one else is watching.

The second layer is accountability to your spouse, if you're married. Your wife sees you more consistently than anyone else. She knows the gap between your public persona and your private reality. A healthy marriage includes mutual accountability, the willingness to hear her observations about your life and take them seriously, even when they're uncomfortable. Many men treat their wives as someone to manage rather than someone who can speak truth into their lives. This is a significant loss.

The third layer is accountability to a mentor or spiritual father, someone further down the road who can offer wisdom from experience, see patterns you can't see, and challenge you from a position of demonstrated faithfulness. This is someone who has authority in your life because of their track record, someone whose correction you receive because you trust their character.

The fourth layer is accountability to peers, brothers walking the same road, fighting the same battles, pursuing the same growth. This is the accountability described in Galatians:

"Carry each other's burdens, and in this way you will fulfill the law of Christ."
Galatians 6:2

Burden-bearing is mutual. You carry theirs; they carry yours. This isn't a hierarchy but a partnership, men standing together because none of them are strong enough to stand alone. Peer accountability has a different texture than mentorship:

it's characterized by mutuality, shared struggle, and the knowledge that you're in the same fight.

Most men need all four layers operating simultaneously. Accountability to God keeps you honest when no one else is watching. Accountability to your spouse keeps your home life from drifting while you're busy elsewhere. Accountability to a mentor provides wisdom and correction from someone who sees further than you can. Accountability to brothers provides the daily support and challenge of men in the same trenches.

Building What You Need

Many men agree they need accountability but don't know how to find or build it. The concept seems valuable in theory but impossible to implement in practice. Here's how to actually build the accountability relationships you need.

First, identify the right person. Not everyone makes a good accountability partner. You're looking for someone who demonstrates trustworthiness through their own life, their integrity, their faithfulness, their walk with God. You're looking for someone who will tell you the truth even when it's uncomfortable, who cares more about your growth than about your approval of them. You're looking for someone who has enough distance from your situation to see clearly but enough knowledge of your life to speak specifically.

Second, initiate the conversation directly. Accountability relationships rarely form by accident. Someone has to say, "I need this, and I'm wondering if you'd be willing to walk with me in this way." That vulnerability feels risky, but it's required. Explain what you're looking for: someone to ask you hard questions, check on your progress, speak honestly about what they see. Ask if they'd be willing to meet regularly for this purpose.

Third, establish clear structure. Accountability without structure becomes vague and easily abandoned. Decide how often you'll meet, where, and for how long. Decide what areas of life you'll discuss, spiritual disciplines, marriage, integrity, specific struggles you're addressing. Decide what questions you'll ask each other. The structure creates the container that makes accountability sustainable.

Fourth, commit to radical honesty. Accountability only works if you actually tell the truth. The temptation is to shade your reports, emphasize the positives, minimize the failures, manage how you're perceived. But managed accountability isn't accountability at all, it's performance. You have to decide in advance that you'll tell the whole truth, even when it's embarrassing, even when you'd rather hide.

Fifth, give permission for pursuit. Tell your accountability partner that if you start avoiding, like I did for those three weeks, they have permission to pursue you. Ask them not to accept your excuses, to press when you're deflecting, to show up even when you're making yourself unavailable. This permission, given in a clear moment, protects you in the murky moments when avoidance seems attractive.

Sixth, make it mutual when possible. The best accountability relationships involve both parties being accountable to each other. You're not just receiving accountability; you're providing it. This mutuality creates equality, distributes vulnerability, and prevents the relationship from feeling like surveillance from above.

What Healthy Accountability Looks Like

Not all accountability is healthy. Some accountability relationships damage rather than develop, control rather than cultivate, shame rather than strengthen. Learning to distinguish between healthy and unhealthy accountability protects you from harm while helping you recognize the real thing.

Healthy accountability is rooted in love. The person holding you accountable genuinely cares about your good, not about controlling your behavior or feeling superior to you. Their motivation is your growth, not their power. When they speak hard truth, it comes wrapped in evident care, you can feel that they're for you even when they're challenging you.

Healthy accountability balances truth and grace. Accountability without grace becomes harsh legalism, every failure met with condemnation, every struggle met with judgment. Grace without accountability becomes sloppy permissiveness, affirmation without challenge, acceptance without expectation. God uses both: accountability shapes your discipline while grace restores your strength. A healthy accountability relationship reflects this balance.

Healthy accountability respects your agency. It doesn't make decisions for you or demand compliance. It asks questions, offers perspective, speaks truth, and then respects your freedom to respond. You're not being controlled; you're being challenged. You retain responsibility for your own choices, but you're making those choices with additional input and visibility.

Healthy accountability is confidential. What you share stays between you and the person you've trusted. There's no gossip, no sharing your struggles with others without permission, no using your vulnerabilities against you later. Trust is sacred, and accountability requires trust to function.

Unhealthy accountability, by contrast, is characterized by control, shame, harshness, gossip, power dynamics, or the absence of genuine care. If accountability leaves you feeling condemned rather than convicted, controlled rather than challenged, worse about yourself rather than clearer about your growth, something is wrong. Accountability should produce freedom and strength, not bondage and despair.

If you're in an unhealthy accountability relationship, you may need to address it directly or, if necessary, step away from it. Past experience with unhealthy accountability doesn't mean all accountability is harmful, it means you need to find the healthy version. Don't let bad experiences rob you of what healthy accountability provides.

Ownership Against Victimhood

Accountability stands in direct opposition to the victim mindset that has become pervasive in our culture. Victimhood says, "Life is happening to me, I'm the passive recipient of forces beyond my control." Ownership says, "I control my choices, my responses, my direction."

To be clear: some people are genuinely victims of genuine wrongs. Injustice is real. Abuse is real. Circumstances beyond anyone's control are real. Acknowledging that you were wronged isn't victim mindset, it's honesty. But victim mindset goes further: it makes victimhood an identity, a permanent posture toward life, an explanation for everything that absolves you of any responsibility for your present and future.

Victim mindset says, "People are against me." Ownership says, "Some people may oppose me, but I control how I respond." Victim mindset says, "No one understands my situation." Ownership says, "My situation is challenging, but I'm still responsible for what I do within it." Victim mindset says, "I can't change because of what happened to me." Ownership says, "What happened to me was real, but it doesn't determine what happens through me."

You may not control every event in your life. But you always control your obedience. You always control your choices within your circumstances. You always control whether you move toward God or away from Him. Victimhood kills momentum by convincing you that movement is impossible. Ownership creates momentum by reminding you that you're an agent, not just a recipient.

Accountability reinforces ownership by consistently asking: What are you going to do? Not what happened to you, not what others did wrong, not what circumstances made difficult, but what are you going to do with what you control? This question, asked regularly, trains you to think like an owner rather than a victim, an agent rather than a passive recipient.

The Man Accountability Builds

A man who embraces accountability becomes someone God can trust with responsibility and someone others want to follow.

God entrusts influence to men who steward their lives well. A man who avoids accountability becomes unpredictable, you never know which version of him will show up because he has no external checks on his drift. But a man who embraces accountability becomes dependable. He finishes what he starts because someone's asking about it. He follows through on commitments because he knows he'll have to account for them. He owns his decisions rather than blaming circumstances. He corrects his mistakes rather than hiding them. He learns quickly because correction is a regular part of his life.

These are the men God can trust with responsibility. These are the men people follow. These are the men who win in the arena, not because they never fail, but because they never stop being accountable for their failures and their growth.

A man with nothing to hide has nothing to fear. He's brought his weaknesses into the light, so they can't be used against him. He's been honest about his failures, so exposure holds no terror. He lives in the freedom that comes from walking in truth rather than managing an image. This freedom makes him unshakeable in ways that the hiding man can never be.

"From everyone who has been given much, much will be demanded; and from the one who has been entrusted with much, much more will be asked." Luke 12:48

If you've been given much, and you have, much will be required. This isn't a threat but an invitation: step into the responsibility that matches your gifts. Take ownership of what you've been given. Embrace the accountability that ensures you steward it well. The man who takes responsibility for everything he can control discovers that God takes responsibility for everything he can't. That partnership, your ownership joined to His sovereignty, is the foundation of real strength.

* * *

That friend who showed up at my house after three weeks of my avoidance did me one of the greatest kindnesses anyone has ever done.

He refused to let me hide. He pursued me when I was running. He asked the hard question and waited for the honest answer. And in doing so, he caught a drift that would have become a disaster if left unaddressed.

That's what accountability is: love expressed as pursuit, truth delivered with grace, strength offered to weakness. It's not punishment, it's partnership. It's not surveillance, it's support. It's not about catching you in failure; it's about keeping you aligned with who you're becoming.

So here's the question I want you to sit with:

Who has permission to ask you the hard questions, and when did they lastask?

If no one comes to mind, that absence is your most urgent next step. Find someone. Initiate the conversation. Build what you need. If someone does come to mind but you've been avoiding them, like I avoided my friend, that avoidance is a signal that something needs light. Make the call. Have the conversation. Let them do what accountability is designed to do.

The arena rewards men who take ownership. Responsibility isn't a burden, it's power. And accountability is the structure that ensures your power serves your purpose rather than sabotaging it.

Ownership is the key that unlocks the next level of your life. Stop hiding. Start owning. And invite others into the process, because you weren't designed to carry it alone.

CHAPTER NINE

Interest vs. Commitment

"Suppose one of you wants to build a tower. Won't you first sit down and estimate the cost to see if you have enough money to complete it?"

(Luke 14:28)

* * *

I had a shelf full of books I'd never finished.

Leadership books, spiritual formation books, books about discipline and habits and becoming the man I knew I should become. I'd purchased each one with enthusiasm, started each one with intention, gotten halfway through each one feeling inspired, and then set each one aside when the next urgent thing demanded attention. The pattern was so consistent it had become invisible to me. I was a collector of good ideas, not a practitioner of them.

My life reflected the same pattern. I had started exercise programs that faded within weeks. I had committed to morning routines that lasted until the first disruption. I had declared new priorities that quietly returned to their old positions as soon as the initial motivation wore off. I had the vocabulary of transformation without its substance. I knew what I should be doing; I just wasn't doing it with any consistency.

Then a mentor said something that exposed the truth I'd been avoiding: "You're interested in change. You're not committed to it. And there's a vast difference between the two."

I wanted to argue. I wanted to point to all my efforts, all my good intentions, all the books on my shelf as evidence of my seriousness. But he just looked at me and asked a simple question: "What have you actually sacrificed for the change you say you want?"

I didn't have an answer. I had sacrificed nothing. I had added things, books, programs, plans, but I had given up nothing. My comfort remained intact. My convenience remained protected. My excuses remained active. I had been trying to add transformation to my existing life rather than restructuring my life around transformation. And that, my mentor explained, is the difference between interest and commitment.

Interest adds. Commitment sacrifices. Interest fits change into whatever space remains after you've protected everything else. Commitment rearranges everything else to make space for change. Interest is cheap; commitment is costly. And the cost is precisely what separates the men who transform from the men who merely wish they would.

That conversation began the most important shift of my adult life. I stopped adding and started sacrificing. I stopped collecting ideas and started implementing them, one at a time, with whatever cost they required. The transformation I had been chasing for years finally began, not because I wanted it more, but because I was finally willing to pay for it.

The Distinction That Changes Everything

Most men are interested in becoming better. They're interested in stronger marriages, deeper faith, greater discipline, more effective leadership. Interest is everywhere. It fills conferences and book sales and New Year's resolutions. Interest is the default state of any man who has glimpsed the gap between who he is and who he could be.

But few men are committed. Commitment is rare precisely because it's costly, and most men aren't willing to pay. They want the results without the process, the reward without the repetition, the transformation without the sacrifice. They're interested in what commitment produces but not in what commitment requires.

Interest talks about change; commitment builds it. Interest likes the idea of discipline; commitment maintains discipline when the idea has lost its appeal.

Interest shows up when conditions are favorable; commitment shows up regardless of conditions. Interest depends on motivation; commitment depends on decision.

Interest fades when difficulty arrives; commitment endures through difficulty because difficulty was already factored into the cost.

Jesus understood this distinction and addressed it directly. Before inviting followers into costly discipleship, He warned them to count the cost:

"Suppose one of you wants to build a tower. Won't you first sit down and estimate the cost to see if you have enough money to complete it? For if you lay the foundation and are not able to finish it, everyone who sees it will ridicule you, saying, 'This person began to build and wasn't able to finish.'"
Luke 14:28-30

Jesus wasn't trying to discourage followers, He was trying to produce committed ones rather than merely interested ones. The man who counts the cost and then commits has something the man who starts enthusiastically without counting lacks: the knowledge that he's chosen this despite the price, and the determination that comes from that informed choice. Interest begins without counting; commitment counts first and then begins with full knowledge of what's required.

The arena doesn't respond to interested men. It exposes them. When pressure arrives, and it always arrives, interest disappears. The man who started enthusiastically discovers that his enthusiasm was conditional on circumstances he no longer has. But committed men endure the pressure because they knew it was coming. They counted the cost, decided to pay it, and aren't surprised when the bill comes due.

Why Interest Always Fails

Interest fails because it depends on conditions that never remain favorable. Interest says, "I'll start when I feel ready" but you never feel ready enough to sustain action through difficulty. Interest says, "I'll do it when I have more time" but more time never materializes, and if it did, new demands would fill it. Interest says, "I'll get serious when things slow down" but things never slow down for the interested man. They just expose him.

The fundamental problem with interest is that it's a feeling, and feelings are unreliable foundations for sustained action. Interest fluctuates with mood, energy,

circumstances, and the passing of initial enthusiasm. The book that excited you last week sits unfinished this week because the feeling faded. The program you started with energy last month lies abandoned this month because energy is not commitment.

Commitment, by contrast, is not a feeling, it's a decision. Commitment doesn't care about your mood; it acts despite your mood. Commitment doesn't negotiate with excuses; it acknowledges their existence and moves anyway.

Commitment doesn't depend on motivation; it generates motivation through action rather than waiting for motivation to generate action. Commitment chooses direction first and allows emotions to follow later, or not. The emotions don't matter. The decision does.

This is why Chapter Seven's emphasis on habits matters so much. Habits are the mechanism through which commitment expresses itself. A committed man doesn't rely on feeling like doing the right thing; he's built systems that ensure he does the right thing regardless of feeling. His commitment has become embodied in routines that don't require daily renegotiation. The interested man has to decide every day whether to follow through; the committed man decided once and built structures that carry the decision forward.

Interest asks for permission, from circumstances, from feelings, from perfect conditions that never arrive. Commitment takes ownership, of whatever circumstances exist, whatever feelings are present, whatever imperfect conditions reality has provided. The interested man waits for the right moment. The committed man works with this moment, because this moment is all anyone ever actually has.

What Commitment Actually Requires

Commitment requires sacrifice, actual sacrifice, not just the willingness to sacrifice if it ever becomes necessary. The interested man protects everything while hoping to add transformation. The committed man understands that transformation requires subtraction: removing what stands in the way, eliminating what competes for energy and attention, giving up what's incompatible with who you're becoming.

My mentor's question exposed exactly this gap in my life: "What have you actually sacrificed?" Not what are you willing to sacrifice theoretically, but what have you actually given up? The answer revealed my level of commitment far more accurately than any declaration I could make. I had sacrificed nothing because I had committed to nothing, regardless of what I told myself about my seriousness.

Commitment requires sacrificing comfort. Growth happens outside your comfort zone; staying comfortable ensures you stay the same. The committed man has made peace with discomfort because he's chosen a destination worth being uncomfortable for. The interested man keeps trying to find a comfortable path to an uncomfortable destination, and such a path doesn't exist.

Commitment requires sacrificing convenience. The right thing is rarely the convenient thing. The committed man does it anyway, not because he enjoys inconvenience but because he's valued the outcome above the ease. The interested man keeps waiting for the right thing to also become the convenient thing, and it never does.

Commitment requires sacrificing ego. Growth requires admitting what you don't know, acknowledging where you've failed, receiving correction without defensiveness. The committed man has subordinated his ego to his development. The interested man protects his ego while hoping to somehow develop without the exposure that development requires.

Jesus made the cost explicit:

"Whoever wants to be my disciple must deny themselves and take up their cross daily and follow me." Luke 9:23

Notice the daily nature of the requirement. This isn't a one-time sacrifice that settles the matter forever. It's daily denial, daily cross-bearing, daily following.

Commitment isn't a moment of decision that you can then coast on; it's a posture of ongoing sacrifice that must be renewed each day. The committed man doesn't just decide once, he decides again every morning, and his life reflects the accumulation of those daily decisions.

What you're willing to give up reveals what you truly want. If you're unwilling to sacrifice comfort, you want comfort more than growth. If you're unwilling to

sacrifice convenience, you want convenience more than calling. If you're unwilling to sacrifice ego, you want to feel good about yourself more than you want to actually become good. The sacrifice clarifies the priority, not in theory, but in reality.

Commitment and Everything You've Learned

This book has walked you through a comprehensive framework for transformation: the call to enter the arena rather than watch from the stands, the necessity of establishing identity before strategy, the reality of the fight within, the disciplines of confession and correction, the battle against fear, doubt, and comparison, the practice of intentional living, the importance of daily habits, and the power of accountability as ownership. You now have knowledge. The question is whether you're interested in that knowledge or committed to implementing it.

Think about Chapter One's call to enter the arena. Are you interested in the idea of being a man of action rather than a spectator, or are you committed to actually stepping off the sidelines into whatever arena God has placed before you? Interest admires the concept; commitment enters despite the fear.

Think about Chapter Two's framework of identity before strategy. Are you interested in understanding who God says you are, or are you committed to the ongoing work of letting that identity replace the false identities you've constructed? Interest appreciates the theology; commitment does the soul work of genuine identity formation.

Think about Chapter Three's exposure of the fight within. Are you interested in acknowledging that you have internal battles, or are you committed to fighting them daily, with the weapons available, refusing to let them win? Interest admits the struggle; commitment engages it with everything you have.

Think about Chapter Four's disciplines of confession and correction. Are you interested in the concept of bringing hidden things into the light, or are you committed to actually confessing what you've been hiding to the brothers who can help you? Interest values transparency theoretically; commitment speaks the uncomfortable truth out loud.

Think about Chapter Five's battle against fear, doubt, and comparison. Are you interested in overcoming these enemies, or are you committed to refusing their vote on your obedience, moving despite their voices, acting when they're screaming at you to stay still? Interest hopes they'll go away; commitment moves regardless.

Think about Chapter Six's practice of intentional living. Are you interested in living with purpose rather than drifting, or are you committed to building the structures, making the decisions, and maintaining the focus that intentionality requires? Interest dislikes drift; commitment builds systems to prevent it.

Think about Chapter Seven's emphasis on daily habits. Are you interested in the idea that habits shape who you become, or are you committed to actually building the specific habits that will form you into the man God is calling you to be? Interest agrees with the principle; commitment implements the practice.

Think about Chapter Eight's call to accountability as ownership. Are you interested in having people who hold you accountable, or are you committed to finding those people, initiating those conversations, and giving them permission to pursue you when you're hiding? Interest appreciates accountability; commitment builds it into your life.

Everything in this book is useless if you're merely interested. Everything in this book becomes transformative if you're committed. The content hasn't changed between those two scenarios, only your relationship to it has.

Moving From Interest to Commitment

If you recognize yourself as having been merely interested, as I was with my shelf of unfinished books, the question becomes: how do you make the shift to genuine commitment? It's not enough to simply decide to be more committed; interest has made that decision many times and failed to follow through. Something more is required.

First, count the cost honestly. What will actual transformation require you to give up? Not in vague terms, specifically. What comfort will you sacrifice? What time will you reallocate? What habits will you break? What excuses will you stop accepting

from yourself? Write these down. Look at them. Decide whether you're willing to pay, knowing exactly what payment means. Jesus told people to count the cost because informed commitment is more durable than enthusiastic ignorance.

Second, start with one commitment, not many. Interest spreads attention across many things superficially. Commitment focuses attention on one thing deeply. Choose the single most important change from everything this book has presented, the one that would have the greatest impact on your life, and commit to that one thing fully. Let it be your proving ground. When you've demonstrated commitment there, you can expand. But starting with everything ensures you'll commit to nothing.

Third, make your commitment public. Interest hides because exposure creates accountability. Commitment declares itself because accountability strengthens resolve. Tell someone, a brother, a mentor, your spouse, exactly what you're committing to and exactly what it will cost. Give them permission to ask you about it. Let the knowledge that someone else knows add weight to your decision.

Fourth, build structures that assume commitment. Don't wait to feel committed before acting committed. Schedule the time. Remove the obstacles. Create the environment. Build the habits. Let the structures carry you when motivation fades, because motivation will fade, and structures will remain. The committed man doesn't trust himself to always feel like following through; he builds systems that make following through the path of least resistance.

Fifth, expect the test and prepare for it. Commitment is tested, not merely claimed. At some point, probably sooner than you'd like, circumstances will challenge whether you're actually committed or merely interested. The test might be fatigue, discouragement, competing demands, lack of visible progress, or simple boredom. Know that this test is coming. Decide in advance that you'll pass it. When it arrives, recognize it for what it is: the crucible that proves whether your commitment was genuine.

What Commitment Produces

The cost of commitment is real, but so is the return. Commitment produces what interest can only imagine.

Commitment produces consistency, the quality that separates those who transform from those who merely intend to. Consistent men don't drift because their commitment anchors them. They don't panic because their commitment has prepared them. They don't crumble because their commitment has strengthened them. They don't chase shortcuts because their commitment has taught them that shortcuts don't lead where they want to go. Consistency is the compound interest of character, and commitment is what makes the deposits.

Commitment produces simplicity. When you're committed, decisions become simple because your commitments have already made them for you. You stop wondering whether you feel like doing the right thing;

you do the right thing because you're committed to it. The mental energy wasted on daily renegotiation becomes available for actual progress. Life simplifies when commitment eliminates the options you've already decided against.

Commitment produces authority. Authority is not charisma; it's consistency.

When you're committed to truth, people learn they can trust what you say. When you're committed to discipline, people see they can rely on your follow-through. When you're committed to your calling, people sense they're in the presence of someone who knows who he is and where he's going. Authority flows naturally from the demonstrated commitment that others can observe over time.

And commitment produces the attention of God. Scripture is filled with men God blessed not because they were perfect but because they were committed. Noah kept building when everyone mocked him. Abraham kept trusting when the promise seemed impossible. Joseph kept serving with integrity when circumstances were unjust. David kept repenting when his failures were grievous. Paul kept preaching when opposition was fierce. These weren't perfect men, they were committed men. And commitment, not perfection, is what God honors.

"Let us run with perseverance the race marked out for us, fixing our eyes on Jesus, the pioneer and perfecter of faith."
Hebrews 12:1-2

The race requires perseverance, sustained commitment over time, not bursts of enthusiasm that fade. The cloud of witnesses who have gone before were marked by this quality: they kept going. They endured. They committed and didn't turn back. The race marked out for you requires the same. Not perfection, perseverance. Not flawless performance, faithful commitment. Not interest, but the costly decision to keep running regardless of what the running costs.

The Question That Remains

The arena belongs to committed men. It always has. Interested men enter and then leave when the cost becomes clear. They quit when it gets messy, collapse when it gets heavy, disappear when it gets real. The arena exposes them, and they retreat to the safety of the stands where observation requires nothing.

But committed men endure. They build. They rise after falling. They fight when fighting is hard. They finish what they started because they counted the cost before starting and decided the destination was worth the price. Commitment is their anchor when storms come, their strength when energy fades, their separation from the many who wanted the same things but weren't willing to pay.

You've read this book. You've encountered its ideas. You've felt whatever you've felt in response to its challenges. But feeling is interest, and interest changes nothing. The only question that matters now is what you're going to do.

Are you going to set this book beside the others on your shelf, appreciated, agreed with, ultimately ignored? Are you going to carry good intentions into the same life you were living before, hoping somehow that exposure to truth will transform you without requiring anything of you? Are you going to remain interested while staying uncommitted, adding this to your collection of inspiration that never became implementation?

Or are you going to decide, today, now, before the feeling fades, that you're done being interested and ready to be committed? Are you going to count the cost, accept it, and pay it? Are you going to choose one thing from this book and pursue it with everything you have until it's built into who you are? Are you going to tell someone what you've decided and give them permission to hold you to it?

The difference between the man you are and the man you could become isn't knowledge, you have enough knowledge. It isn't desire, you want it enough. The difference is commitment. The single variable that determines whether this book changes your life or merely occupied your attention for a season.

* * *

My shelf of unfinished books eventually became my library of implemented ideas, not all at once, but one commitment at a time. The transformation I'd been chasing finally arrived when I stopped adding and started sacrificing, stopped intending and started deciding, stopped being interested and became committed.

The same transformation is available to you. The arena is waiting. The tools have been given. The path has been marked. Everything you need to become the man God is calling you to be has been provided.

So here's the question I want you to sit with, the question that will determine whether this book mattered:

Are you interested, or are you committed, and what will you do in the next twenty-four hours that proves your answer?

Interest talks. Commitment acts. The next day will reveal which one you've chosen.

Choose commitment. Pay the cost. Enter the arena. And become the man you were created to be.

The arena is waiting.

CHAPTER TEN

Greatness in the Moment

"Whatever you do, work at it with all your heart, as working for the Lord, not for human masters."

Colossians 3:23

* * *

The moment that changed everything looked nothing like I expected.

I had imagined that the defining moments of my life would announce themselves, dramatic, unmistakable, obviously significant. I expected trumpets, or at least a clear sense that something important was happening. Instead, the moment that redirected my entire trajectory came disguised as an ordinary Tuesday morning, when I was tired and distracted and completely unaware that anything consequential was at stake.

I had promised to meet with a younger man who wanted to talk about his struggling marriage. The appointment wasn't convenient. I had slept poorly, had a full day ahead, and frankly didn't feel like I had anything useful to offer. Everything in me wanted to reschedule, to push the conversation to a day when I felt more prepared, more present, more capable of being helpful.

But I had made a commitment, and commitments, as we discussed in the previous chapter, don't negotiate with feelings. So I showed up. I listened. I shared what little wisdom I had. The conversation lasted about an hour, and when it ended, I didn't think much of it. I had kept my word. I had been present. That was all.

Years later, that man told me that conversation had saved his marriage. That single hour, which I had almost canceled, which felt unremarkable while it was happening, which I barely remembered, had become a turning point for his entire family. His children would grow up in an intact home because of something I almost didn't do on a morning when I didn't feel ready.

That's when I understood: greatness doesn't announce itself. It hides in ordinary moments that feel insignificant while they're happening. The conversations you almost skip, the commitments you almost break, the small obediences you almost neglect, these are where your life is actually being built. Everyone wants to be great in some imagined future. Few choose to be great in the unremarkable moment right in front of them.

The arena, it turns out, isn't a single dramatic battle. It's a thousand small moments where you choose, often without realizing the stakes, whether to show up or retreat, whether to obey or defer, whether to be present or check out. The man who masters these moments becomes the man who masters his life.

Redefining Greatness

Before we go further, we need to clarify what greatness actually means, because the word carries baggage that could mislead you.

The world defines greatness as achievement, recognition, impact at scale. The great man, in worldly terms, is the one whose name is known, whose accomplishments are celebrated, whose influence extends across many people. This definition creates a problem: by its logic, most men cannot be great, because most men will never be famous, celebrated, or widely influential. If greatness requires platform, most men are disqualified from the start.

But Scripture offers a radically different definition. When the disciples argued about who among them was the greatest, Jesus responded in a way that inverted their entire framework:

"Whoever wants to become great among you must be your servant, and whoever wants to be first must be slave of all."
Mark 10:43-44

Greatness, in Jesus' definition, is not about position but about posture. Not about how many people know your name but about how faithfully you serve. Not about accomplishing impressive things but about being faithful in whatever you've been given. This definition democratizes greatness: the man serving his family in obscurity can be as great as the man leading nations, because greatness is measured by faithfulness rather than by fame.

This reframe is liberating. You don't have to wait for a bigger platform to be great. You don't have to achieve some threshold of recognition before your life counts. Greatness is available right now, in this moment, in whatever sphere God has placed you. The question isn't whether you have the opportunity for greatness, you do. The question is whether you'll choose greatness in the opportunity before you.

Greatness, then, is faithful obedience to whatever God has put in front of you, not someday, but today. Not in theory, but in practice. Not when you feel ready, but right now, with whatever readiness you have. It's showing up fully, serving genuinely, and doing the next right thing regardless of whether anyone notices or applauds. This is the greatness available in every moment to every man willing to choose it.

Why Moments Matter More Than Seasons

People wait for the right season, the season when they'll have more time, more energy, more clarity, more resources. They imagine that transformation happens in seasons of concentrated focus rather than in the daily moments that make up ordinary life.

But seasons don't shape you. Moments do. Seasons are made of moments, and it's in the moments that you actually decide who you are. The decision to pray when you don't feel like it, that's a moment. The choice to tell the truth when a lie would be easier, that's a moment. The commitment to stay present with your family when work is pulling at your attention, that's a moment. These moments are where your character is forged, regardless of what season you're in.

This is why Jesus' teaching on faithfulness focuses on the small and immediate rather than the large and future:

"Whoever can be trusted with very little can also be trusted with much, and whoever is dishonest with very little will also be dishonest with much." Luke 16:10

The "very little" is the moment in front of you. The small choice no one sees.

The minor decision that seems inconsequential. God uses these as the testing ground for everything else. How you handle the very little reveals how you would handle much. And how you handle this moment reveals the man you're becoming across all your moments.

You don't become strong in a season. You become strong in a moment, a moment where you choose strength instead of weakness, and then you repeat that choice until it becomes natural. The first time you choose strength, it's difficult. The hundredth time, it's becoming who you are. Character is formed through accumulated moments, not through waiting for the right season to begin.

This means the moment you're in right now matters. Not the moment you're planning for, not the season you're hoping will come, but this one, the one where you're reading these words, the one you'll step into when you set this book down.

That moment is where your greatness will be built or squandered.

The Weapon of Presence

To choose greatness in the moment, you must first be present in the moment. This sounds obvious but has become increasingly rare. Most men move through their days distracted, checked out, mentally somewhere other than where they physically are.

You've experienced this. You've been in conversations where the other person's eyes kept drifting to their phone, where you could tell their mind was elsewhere, where you were physically in the same room but not actually together. And you've been that person, present in body while absent in attention, going through motions while your mind ran through worries, plans, or distractions.

Presence is a weapon precisely because it's so rare. When you're truly present, fully attentive to where you are and who you're with, you see opportunities others miss. You notice the subtle cues that indicate someone is struggling. You hear the Holy Spirit's prompting that gets drowned out by mental noise. You recognize the moment where strength is required rather than sleepwalking through it. Presence turns ordinary moments into opportunities for obedience that the distracted man never even notices.

Cultivating presence requires intentional practice. It means putting the phone away, not just silencing it. It means training your mind to return to the present when it wanders to the future or past. It means deciding, before entering a conversation or situation, that you will be fully there. It means building habits, like the morning disciplines we discussed in Chapter Seven, that anchor your attention rather than scatter it.

Greatness demands presence because presence is where obedience actually happens. You cannot obey in a moment you're not present to. You cannot choose faithfulness in a situation you're not paying attention to. The man who is mentally elsewhere is incapable of greatness here, regardless of what he might accomplish in the imaginary future he's distracted by.

The Small Yes That Transforms

Everyone romanticizes the big yes. The dramatic commitment. The bold declaration. "Yes, God, I'll go anywhere. I'll do anything. Use me however You want." These moments feel significant, and they can be. But they're not where transformation actually happens.

The small yes is harder, and more important. The small yes is saying "yes, I'll pray" when you don't feel like praying. It's saying "yes, I'll speak truth" when truth is uncomfortable. It's saying "yes, I'll stay disciplined" when no one is checking whether you do. It's saying "yes, I'll hold my tongue" when pride wants to speak. It's saying "yes, I'll forgive" when you'd rather stay bitter.

The small yes builds what the big yes can only declare. You can make a grand commitment to follow God anywhere, but if you won't follow Him in the small obedience of this ordinary moment, the grand commitment is theater. The small yes is the proof that the big yes was genuine. It's where commitment from Chapter Nine gets demonstrated rather than merely claimed.

Paul understood that all of life, every mundane action, every ordinary moment, is an arena for faithfulness:

"So whether you eat or drink or whatever you do, do it all for the glory of God."
1 Corinthians 10:31

Whatever you do. Not just the spiritual activities. Not just the impressive moments. Whatever you do, including the eating and drinking, the commuting and working, the ordinary rhythms of daily life. All of it can be done for God's glory, which means all of it is an opportunity for faithfulness, which means all of it is an arena for greatness. The small yes to do this ordinary thing with intention and integrity is a spiritual act that compounds over time into something far greater than any single dramatic gesture.

What Pressure Actually Reveals

We discussed in Chapter Seven that you don't rise to the occasion, you fall to the level of your habits. This principle applies directly to moments of pressure. The moment doesn't build you; it reveals what your accumulated moments have already built.

When the crisis comes, and it will, your training shows. Your habits show.

Your discipline shows. Your faith shows. The pressure strips away pretense and reveals what's actually underneath. The man who has been great in hidden moments will be great in visible ones. The man who has been cutting corners when no one was watching will cut them when everyone is.

This is why greatness in the mundane matters so much. The mundane is your training ground for the momentous. Every small choice you make when nothing seems at stake is preparing you for the choices you'll make when everything is on the line.

Faithfulness in little is practice for faithfulness in much. Excellence in the unseen is preparation for excellence in the spotlight.

The enemy understands this, which is why he attacks in moments rather than waiting for grand battles. A moment of loneliness when you're tempted to seek comfort in the wrong place. A moment of fatigue when your defenses are down. A moment of frustration when you're tempted to say something you can't take back. A moment of pride when you're tempted to take credit that belongs elsewhere. These moments are where spiritual warfare is actually fought, not in dramatic confrontations but in the small choices that seem inconsequential until you realize they've shaped who you've become.

You win spiritual warfare in the moment you decide whose voice you obey.

When fear speaks and faith speaks, and you choose faith, that's victory. When flesh speaks and Spirit speaks, and you choose Spirit, that's victory. When the easy path and the right path diverge, and you choose the right path, that's victory. These victories, accumulated across thousands of moments, make you the man who can stand when greater tests arrive.

Where Everything Comes Together

Everything this book has taught you comes together in moments. The concepts aren't separate compartments; they're integrated in the living reality of each choice you make.

Your identity from Chapter Two is expressed in moments. When you face a choice, you're either living out of who God says you are or reverting to the false identities you've constructed. Every moment is an opportunity to act from your true identity, or to forget it.

The fight within from Chapter Three is engaged in moments. The battle between flesh and Spirit, between the man you're becoming and the patterns that want to pull you back, this battle is fought in the immediate choices of daily life, not in some abstract spiritual realm.

Confession and correction from Chapter Four happen in moments, the moment you choose to speak truth about a failure rather than hide it, the moment you receive a brother's correction rather than defending yourself.

Fear, doubt, and comparison from Chapter Five attack in moments, a moment of uncertainty when you're tempted to retreat, a moment of scrolling when comparison steals your peace. You defeat these enemies or succumb to them in real-time moments, not in theoretical battles.

Intentional living from Chapter Six is lived out moment by moment. The structures you build create the context, but the actual living happens in each moment as you choose alignment or drift.

The habits from Chapter Seven are built in moments, each time you do the thing you've committed to do, you're strengthening the habit in that specific moment.

Accountability from Chapter Eight creates moments of honesty, the moment when your brother asks a hard question and you choose to answer truthfully.

Commitment from Chapter Nine is proven in moments, not in the declaration but in the follow-through, not in the intention but in the action when the moment requires it.

The arena is not a single battlefield. It's a collection of moments strung together into a life. You don't win once and celebrate forever. You win moment by moment, choice by choice, day by day. The man who understands this stops waiting for the big battle and starts showing up fully for each small one.

The Arena Is Now

We've come full circle. Chapter One called you into the arena, to stop watching from the stands and enter the place where life is actually lived. Now, at the end of this journey, I want you to understand where the arena actually is.

The arena is not somewhere you'll arrive someday when you're more ready.

The arena is now. This moment. This choice. This opportunity to be faithful or unfaithful, present or absent, great or mediocre. You don't prepare for the arena and then enter it later; you're already in it, and every moment is asking what you'll do.

The arena is the conversation with your wife tonight. It's the work you'll do tomorrow when no one is checking. It's how you'll respond the next time you're frustrated, tempted, tired, or tested. It's the small yes or the small no that seems to carry no weight but actually carries more weight than you realize.

Roosevelt's words from Chapter One ring differently now. The man in the arena, whose face is marred by dust and sweat and blood, he's not in some distant battle. He's in the dust and sweat and blood of ordinary life lived faithfully. He's in the early morning when getting up is hard and discipline calls anyway. He's in the evening when presence with family requires more than collapse on the couch. He's in the moment of temptation when no one would know if he gave in. The arena is everywhere, all the time, for anyone willing to show up.

Greatness, then, doesn't show up later. It shows up now, or it doesn't show up at all. The man who will be great tomorrow is the man being faithful today. The future you're building is being constructed right now, in this moment and the next and the one after that. There is no later where the real work begins. The real work has already begun, and you're either doing it or avoiding it.

* * *

That conversation I almost skipped, the one that helped save a marriage, taught me something I've never forgotten. I had no idea, in the moment, that anything significant was happening. It felt ordinary. I was tired and underprepared and doubtful that I had anything useful to offer. But I showed up anyway, because I had committed to showing up, and commitment doesn't ask how you feel.

That's how most of life works. You rarely know, in the moment, which moments will matter most. You can't predict which conversation will change someone's trajectory, which small obedience will compound into something significant, which ordinary Tuesday will become the hinge on which something important turns. All you can do is show up, fully present, faithfully obedient, trusting that God is doing something in the moments you can't see.

You've read this entire book. You've encountered its ideas, felt its challenges, perhaps even made some decisions. But the book doesn't matter. What matters is what you do when you set it down, the next moment, and the one after that, and the thousands of moments that will make up the rest of your life.

You are not the sum of your potential. You are not the sum of your intentions. You are not the sum of your feelings about who you want to become. You are the sum of your moments, the accumulated weight of every small choice you've made and will make. The man you're becoming is being built right now, whether you're paying attention or not.

So here's the question I want you to sit with, the question that closes this book and opens the rest of your life:

What is the next moment in front of you, and what does greatness look like in it?

Not someday. Not when you're ready. Not when circumstances

improve. Now. The very next moment after you finish reading these words. What does faithfulness look like there? What does presence require? What does obedience demand?

The arena is waiting. It's been waiting this whole time. But it's not somewhere you go, it's where you already are.

Enter it fully.

Stay present.

Choose greatness in this moment, and then the next, and then the next. That's the only way it's ever been done. Welcome to the arena.

CHAPTER ELEVEN

The Discipline of Focus

"I am doing a great work and cannot come down."

(Nehemiah 6:3)

* * *

I was drowning in good opportunities.

On paper, everything looked impressive. I was involved in multiple initiatives, serving on boards, attending meetings, saying yes to requests that seemed reasonable and even important. My calendar was full. My reputation was that of someone who showed up, who could be counted on, who was willing to help. By every external measure, I was succeeding.

But something was breaking. The things that mattered most to me, my family, my primary calling, my own soul, were getting the scraps. I had time and energy for everyone else's priorities but not for my own. I was present everywhere and effective nowhere. The breadth of my involvement was producing shallowness in everything I touched. I was spread so thin that nothing was getting my best.

The turning point came when I realized a devastating truth: every yes costs something. Every commitment I made to one thing was a commitment I couldn't make to something else. My yeses to good things were actually nos to essential things. I wasn't failing because I was lazy or undisciplined; I was failing because I was unfocused. I had confused activity with impact, busyness with faithfulness, presence with effectiveness.

Learning to focus, to say no to good things so I could say yes to essential things, transformed my life. It felt counterintuitive at first, even selfish. But I discovered that focus isn't selfishness; it's stewardship. The man who tries to do everything does nothing well. The man who focuses his energy on what matters most produces impact that the scattered man never can.

The Myth of Balance

We've been sold a lie called balance. The idea sounds reasonable: give equal attention to all areas of life, keep everything in proportion, don't let any one thing dominate.

But balance, as it's commonly understood, is a recipe for mediocrity. The man who gives equal attention to everything gives exceptional attention to nothing.

Think about anyone who has achieved something significant, in ministry, in business, in art, in any field. Without exception, they were imbalanced. They gave disproportionate attention to their primary calling. They sacrificed good things to pursue essential things. They understood that excellence requires concentration, not distribution. You cannot be world-class at something while giving it the same attention you give everything else.

The biblical model isn't balance, it's priority. Jesus didn't give equal time to every request. He withdrew from crowds to pray. He declined opportunities that didn't align with His mission. He focused on twelve men rather than trying to personally disciple everyone who showed interest. His impact came not from doing everything but from doing the right things with concentrated attention.

What I'm advocating isn't reckless neglect of important responsibilities. Your family matters. Your health matters. Your spiritual life matters. But within those priorities, there's a primary calling, the thing God has specifically assigned to you, and that calling requires disproportionate investment to flourish. Intentional imbalance means choosing where to over-invest rather than spreading yourself so thin that nothing gets what it needs.

The Hidden Cost of Yes

Here's what most people don't understand: every yes is also a no. When you say yes to one thing, you're saying no to something else, even if you don't realize it. Time and energy are finite. Every commitment consumes resources that then aren't for other commitments. The question isn't whether you'll say no; the question is what you'll say no to.

Most men don't ruin their potential through obvious failures. They ruin it through the accumulation of harmless yeses. Each individual commitment seems reasonable, a board to serve on, a project to help with, a meeting to attend, a favor to grant. None of them are bad. Many of them are genuinely good. But accumulated, they consume the margin that focused work requires. Good becomes the enemy of essential.

Consider what your yeses are costing you. That committee you joined, what didn't get your attention because of it? That ongoing commitment you maintain out of obligation, what would you do with that time and energy if it were freed? The requests you keep accepting because you don't want to disappoint people, what's the cost to the people who actually depend on you, who get your leftovers instead of your best?

The most dangerous yeses are the ones that feel productive. They keep you busy. They make you feel needed. They fill your calendar with activity that looks impressive. But activity isn't the same as impact. Busyness isn't the same as faithfulness. The scattered man feels productive while accomplishing little that lasts.

How Jesus Said No

Jesus was constantly surrounded by legitimate needs. People wanted healing, teaching, attention, miracles. Every request was genuine. Every need was real. If anyone could have justified trying to help everyone, it was Jesus. Yet He repeatedly declined legitimate requests to stay focused on His actual mission.

Early in His ministry, after a night of healing many people, the crowds came looking for more. His disciples found Him and said, "Everyone is looking for you!" It was an invitation to return, to meet the demand, to keep doing what had been so effective. But Jesus responded:

"Let us go somewhere else, to the nearby villages, so I can preach there also. That is why I have come." Mark 1:38

“That is why I have come.” Jesus knew His mission, and He protected it. The crowds wanted more of what He'd already given. But His calling wasn't to stay in one place meeting endless demands; it was to preach in many places. Saying no to the crowd's request was saying yes to His actual assignment.

Later, after feeding the five thousand, the crowd wanted to make Jesus king by force. It was an opportunity, influence, power, immediate impact. But John records that Jesus "withdrew again to a mountain by himself." He declined the opportunity because it wasn't aligned with His mission. The path to His kingdom didn't run through popular acclaim; it ran through the cross.

Nehemiah demonstrated the same discipline. While rebuilding Jerusalem's walls, his enemies repeatedly tried to lure him into meetings, into distractions, into anything that would pull him away from his work. His response became a model of focused leadership:

> *"I am doing a great work and cannot come down. Why should the work stop while I leave it and come down to you?"*
> *Nehemiah 6:3*

“I am doing a great work and cannot come down.” That single sentence captures the discipline of focus. Nehemiah knew his assignment. He refused to be pulled from it, even by requests that seemed reasonable, even by people who seemed important, even by opportunities that looked attractive. The wall got built because Nehemiah stayed focused.

Why No Feels So Hard

If focus is so important, why do we struggle so much to maintain it? Why is saying no so difficult? Understanding the resistance helps you overcome it.

We fear disappointing people. The person asking for your time or energy will experience your no as rejection. They may be hurt, frustrated, or confused. We don't want to cause that pain, so we say yes to avoid the discomfort of their disappointment. But consider: you're prioritizing the temporary disappointment of the requester over the lasting disappointment of the people who actually depend on you, your family, those you're called to serve, yourself. Whose disappointment matters more?

We fear missing out. Every opportunity we decline is an experience we won't have, a relationship we won't build, an impact we won't make. But here's the truth: by scattering yourself across many opportunities, you're missing the depth that focus provides. The man who attends every event experiences none of them fully. The man who pursues every opportunity masters none of them. You're already missing out, the question is what you're missing out on.

We fear conflict. Some people don't respond well to no. They push back, argue, try to manipulate. The prospect of that conflict makes yes seem easier. But here's what your inability to say no reveals: people who depend on your yes and resist your no are often the very people you most need boundaries with. Their negative reaction to your boundary is evidence that the boundary was needed.

We fear appearing selfish. Saying no can feel like you're prioritizing yourself over others, like you're being unhelpful or uncaring. But protecting your focus isn't selfishness, it's stewardship. You're guarding the capacity that allows you to fulfill your actual calling. The most generous thing you can do is give your best to what God has assigned you, rather than giving your scraps to everything that asks for your attention.

How to Say No

Knowing that focus matters is different from knowing how to protect it. Here are practical mechanics for saying no in ways that honor both your calling and the people you're declining.

Respond with time, not immediately. When a request comes, your default should be "Let me think about it" rather than an immediate yes. This creates space to evaluate whether the request aligns with your priorities. Many yeses happen simply because we respond before we think. Build in a delay.

Decline without excessive explanation. You don't owe anyone a detailed justification for your no. "I'm not able to commit to that right now" is a complete sentence. Over-explaining often invites negotiation, if you give reasons, people will try to solve around your reasons. A simple, kind, firm no is enough.

Offer an alternative when appropriate. Sometimes you can help without taking on the full request. "I can't join the committee, but I could review documents once a quarter." "I can't lead the project, but I know someone who might be interested." This allows you to maintain relationship and offer genuine help without compromising your focus.

Use existing commitments as your reason. "I've already committed my capacity for this season" is honest and difficult to argue with. Your existing commitments, to your family, your calling, your health, are legitimate reasons that don't require further justification.

Accept that some relationships may be affected. Not everyone will understand your no. Some people may distance themselves when you stop being available for everything they want. That's a cost of focus, but it's also a clarifying process. The relationships that survive your boundaries are the ones built on more than your usefulness.

Practice with small nos before big ones. If you've been a chronic yes-sayer, start small. Decline a minor request. Say no to something low-stakes. Build the muscle before you need it for the major decisions. Each small no makes the next one easier.

Boundaries Versus Selfishness

There's a critical distinction between protecting your focus and being selfish. Not everything can be declined. Some responsibilities are yours whether you chose them or not. Boundaries must be distinguished from abandonment.

Things you can decline: optional invitations that don't align with your priorities, requests that fall outside your calling, opportunities that would overextend your capacity, good things that aren't your things. These can be declined with a clear conscience.

Things you cannot decline: responsibilities God has given you. Your spouse. Your children. Your calling. Your own soul. These aren't optional commitments you can shed for convenience. A man who neglects his family to pursue his career isn't

focused; he's unfaithful. A man who abandons his children to have more personal freedom isn't practicing boundaries; he's abdicating responsibility.

The diagnostic question is this: What am I protecting this time and energy for? If the answer is your calling, your family, your health, your walk with God, that's wisdom. If the answer is your comfort, your entertainment, your avoidance of difficulty, that's selfishness dressed as self-care. Focus protects essential things; selfishness protects easy things.

The man with genuine focus can articulate what he's focused on. He has a clear sense of his primary calling and can explain why certain things get his yes while others get his no. The selfish man can't articulate a calling; he just doesn't want to be bothered. The difference is purpose.

Saying No to Yourself

The hardest nos aren't the ones you say to other people. They're the ones you say to yourself. Your own impulses, appetites, and desires for ease are constantly lobbying for your attention. Focus requires saying no to yourself as often as you say it to others.

The distraction that seems harmless, just a few minutes checking your phone, just a quick scroll through social media, just one more episode, these are requests from yourself that consume focus. They feel insignificant individually but accumulate into hours of lost capacity. Saying no to these small internal requests protects the concentration that meaningful work requires.

Paul described his approach to self-leadership:

> *"No, I strike a blow to my body and make it my slave so that after I have preached to others, I myself will not be disqualified for the prize." 1 Corinthians 9:27*

I make it my slave. Paul didn't let his body, his appetites, his desires, his impulses, dictate his direction. He exercised authority over himself. He said no to himself so that he could say yes to his calling. This is the internal discipline of focus: mastering your own requests before managing everyone else's.

The habits you build, which we discussed earlier, are essentially automated nos to yourself. A morning routine that starts with prayer and Scripture is a no to sleeping in, a no to starting the day with your phone, a no to letting the urgent crowd out the important. Every established habit is a decision you made once and now don't have to make again. The discipline of focus is built through these accumulated nos to yourself.

What Focus Protects

When you maintain focus, when you say no to the good so you can say yes to the essential, you protect things that scattered living destroys.

Focus protects your energy. Every commitment drains capacity. The focused man has reserves because he's not leaking energy in a dozen directions. He brings his full self to what matters because he hasn't depleted himself on what doesn't.

Focus protects your relationships. Your family doesn't get your exhausted leftovers; they get your presence. Your close friends get actual attention rather than distracted half-engagement. The people who matter most receive more because you've declined the people who matter less.

Focus protects your calling. The work God has given you gets the concentration it requires. You're able to go deep rather than staying perpetually shallow. Excellence becomes possible because you're not spreading yourself across so many things that nothing gets what it needs.

Focus protects your soul. You have margin for prayer, for Scripture, for silence, for the spiritual disciplines that keep you healthy. The scattered man is too busy for his own soul; the focused man protects the space his soul requires.

Focus protects your impact. Concentrated effort produces results that scattered effort cannot. The man who focuses his energy like a laser cuts through obstacles that the man who scatters his energy like a floodlight merely illuminates. Impact requires concentration.

* * *

Learning to focus, to embrace intentional imbalance, to say no to good things, to protect my essential calling, was one of the most transformative shifts in my life. It felt wrong at first, like I was abandoning my responsibility to help everyone who asked. But I discovered that by trying to help everyone, I was actually helping no one well. My scattered presence was worth less than my focused absence would have been.

Nehemiah's words have become a filter for me: "I am doing a great work and cannot come down." Not every work is great work. Not every request deserves a yes. Not every opportunity is my opportunity. But the great work, the thing God has specifically assigned to me, that deserves my protection, my focus, my disproportionate investment.

The same is true for you. You have a great work. It may not look impressive to others. It may not come with titles or recognition. But it's yours, your family, your calling, your assignment. And it requires your focus to flourish. Every distraction you entertain, every optional commitment you accept, every request you say yes to out of guilt or obligation, these pull you down from the wall where you belong.

So here's the question I want you to sit with:

What are you currently saying yes to that you know you should decline, and what is it costing you to keep saying yes?

Be honest. You probably already know. There's something, maybe several things, that consume your time and energy while contributing little to your actual calling. They felt reasonable when you agreed to them. They may even be good things. But they're not your things. And they're costing you more than you've admitted.

The discipline of focus requires a decision: Will you continue spreading yourself thin, or will you concentrate your energy on what matters most? Will you keep coming down from the wall for every request, or will you protect your great work?

I am doing a great work and cannot come down.

Let that be your answer too.

Your yes is holy. Protect it.

CHAPTER TWELVE

The Discipline of Standing Firm

"Therefore put on the full armor of God, so that when the day of evil comes, you may be able to stand your ground, and after you have done everything, to stand."

Ephesians 6:13

* * *

The pressure didn't arrive all at once. It accumulated.

First came the financial strain, a business decision that didn't work out the way I'd planned, leaving us in a position far more precarious than we'd ever experienced. Then came the relational conflict, a friendship that had been central to my life fractured in ways I hadn't seen coming, leaving me grieving and confused.

Then came the health scare, test results that required further investigation, weeks of uncertainty while we waited to learn whether something serious was developing.

Each pressure alone would have been manageable. Together, they felt overwhelming. I remember lying awake at night, my mind cycling throughworst-case scenarios, feeling the weight of everything pressing down simultaneously. Every voice inside me was screaming the same thing: retreat. Pull back. Protect yourself. Find an escape route.

What I wanted to do was run, from the financial situation that felt impossible, from the relational pain that felt unbearable, from the health uncertainty that felt terrifying. What I wanted to do was quit, abandon the commitments that now felt too heavy, walk away from the responsibilities that had become crushing, find somewhere quiet where nothing was expected of me.

But something held me. Not my own strength, I had none left. Not my confidence, it had evaporated. What held me was a decision I had made before the pressure arrived: I would not be moved. Not by circumstances, not by emotions, not by fear. I had anchored myself in something deeper than my own capacity to endure, and when everything above the surface was chaos, that anchor held.

Standing firm through that season taught me something I couldn't have learned any other way: standing firm isn't a moment of heroic resolve. It's a discipline, a capacity built through daily practice before pressure arrives and sustained through daily choice while pressure remains. Any man can stand firm when life is quiet. True strength is revealed when everything in your life pushes you to break, retreat, or walk away, and you refuse.

Why Standing Firm Is Rare

Most men stand firm only while conditions remain favorable. They stand when emotions cooperate, when circumstances align, when the path feels smooth, when people approve, when momentum is high. This isn't standing firm, it's standing easy. The difference becomes apparent the moment life pushes back.

When pressure arrives, real pressure, sustained pressure, pressure that doesn't resolve quickly, most men fold. Not because they're weak in character but because they never developed the discipline of standing firm before they needed it. They assumed they would rise to the occasion, only to discover what Chapter Seven taught us about habits: you don't rise to occasions; you fall to the level of your preparation.

This is why Paul's language in Ephesians is so specific. He doesn't merely say "stand" he says "put on the full armor of God, so that when the day of evil comes, you may be able to stand your ground." The armor goes on before the battle. The preparation happens before the pressure. The ability to stand when the day of evil comes depends on what you've done in the days before it arrived.

"Therefore put on the full armor of God, so that when the day of evil comes, you may be able to stand your ground, and after you have done everything, to stand."
Ephesians 6:13

Notice Paul's expectation: there will be a day of evil. Pressure is not a possibility; it's a certainty. The question isn't whether you'll face circumstances that try to move you but whether you'll be prepared when they come. Standing firm is rare because most men never prepare. They assume their current stability is sufficient, until pressure reveals that it wasn't.

The Anchor That Holds

Strength to stand firm doesn't come from personality, willpower, or natural resilience. It comes from your anchor, the thing you're attached to that holds you steady when everything else is shifting.

If your anchor is circumstances, you'll be moved when circumstances change.

If your anchor is relationships, you'll be moved when relationships disappoint. If your anchor is your own resolve, you'll be moved when your resolve exhausts itself. Temporary anchors cannot hold through sustained pressure because they're subject to the same forces that are pressing against you.

The only anchor that holds is something eternal, something outside the shifting circumstances, something unaffected by the pressure bearing down on you. God's character doesn't change when your finances collapse. His Word doesn't shift when your relationships fracture. His promises don't diminish when your health fails. His presence doesn't depart when everything else does.

This is what the psalmist understood:

"God is our refuge and strength, an ever-present help in trouble. Therefore we will not fear, though the earth give way and the mountains fall into the heart of the sea."
Psalm 46:1-2

The psalmist imagines the most extreme possible pressure, the earth itself giving way, mountains falling into the sea, and declares that even then, fear is not necessary. Why? Because God remains refuge and strength regardless of what's happening around you. When your anchor is the unchanging God, you can stand firm through circumstances that would destroy anyone anchored to something lesser.

This connects directly to the identity work we explored in Chapter Two. When you know who God is and who you are in relation to Him, you have an anchor that circumstances cannot cut loose. Your identity doesn't depend on outcomes, so outcomes cannot shake your foundation. Your worth doesn't depend on success, so failure cannot destroy you. Your security doesn't depend on stability, so instability cannot move you. The man rooted in his true identity has something to stand on when everything else falls away.

What Standing Firm Actually Looks Like

Standing firm is not abstract. It has specific shape in specific situations. Understanding what it looks like helps you practice it when pressure comes.

When your marriage is under pressure, standing firm means refusing to walk away, refusing to let difficulty become excuse for abandonment, choosing to work through what's hard rather than flee to what's easy. It means staying in the conversation you'd rather avoid, returning to the counselor even when progress is slow, keeping your vows when keeping them is costly.

When your finances collapse, standing firm means refusing to compromise your integrity, refusing to cut ethical corners to escape the pressure, maintaining your principles even when they make the path harder. It means trusting God's provision while doing the hard work of rebuilding, refusing to let fear drive you to decisions you'd regret.

When your calling seems to be failing, standing firm means refusing to abandon what God assigned you, staying faithful to the work even when results don't come, continuing to obey even when obedience isn't producing what you expected. It means distinguishing between the calling itself and your timeline for its fulfillment, trusting that God's timing is better than your impatience.

When people you trusted betray you, standing firm means refusing to let bitterness take root, processing the pain without letting it poison you, maintaining your character even when others have abandoned theirs. It means forgiving because you've been forgiven, not because they deserve it or because you feel like it.

When your faith is attacked, standing firm means refusing to surrender your convictions, holding to truth even when culture pressures you to compromise, maintaining your confession even when it costs you relationships or opportunities. It means being prepared to give an answer for the hope you have, with gentleness and respect, but without apology.

In each case, standing firm is a decision that must be made repeatedly. It's not one heroic moment but many ordinary ones, waking up each morning and choosing again to hold your ground, refusing again to be moved by what pressed against you yesterday and will press again today.

The Decision That Outlasts the Feeling

Standing firm is a decision, not a feeling. This distinction matters because your feelings will almost never cooperate with the discipline of holding your ground.

Your feelings will scream at you to stop, to slow down, to give up, to protect yourself, to take the easy path. Feelings are designed to seek comfort and avoid pain. When pressure arrives, feelings immediately begin calculating escape routes. If you wait until you feel like standing firm, you'll never stand firm at all.

But your spirit, the part of you anchored in something eternal, whispers something different: keep going, stay faithful, don't move, trust God, keep your footing. The spirit knows what the feelings don't: that retreat leads to worse pain than endurance, that surrender leads to regret that outlasts any temporary relief.

This is the decision-over-emotion principle we explored in Chapter Nine's discussion of commitment. Commitment doesn't care about your mood; it acts despite your mood. Standing firm works the same way. You don't feel like standing firm, you choose to. And you choose again the next day, and the next, until the pressure passes or until you've developed the strength to hold indefinitely.

James understood this dynamic and described its fruit:

> *"Consider it pure joy, my brothers and sisters, whenever you face trials of many kinds, because you know that the testing of your faith produces perseverance. Let perseverance finish its work so that you may be mature and complete, not lacking anything." James 1:2-4*

The testing produces perseverance. Perseverance, allowed to finish its work, produces maturity and completeness. The path to lacking nothing runs through the trials that make you want to quit. Standing firm through the trial is what produces the character you couldn't develop any other way.

The Difference Between Perseverance and Stubbornness

Standing firm is a virtue when you're holding ground God has given you. It becomes a vice when you're refusing to release what God is asking you to surrender.

Discerning the difference requires wisdom that the principle alone cannot provide.

Perseverance holds firm to what is right, what is true, what God has assigned.

Stubbornness holds firm to what you want, what your ego demands, what you've decided regardless of God's direction. Perseverance submits to God while resisting circumstances. Stubbornness resists both God and circumstances, calling rebellion by a spiritual name.

Some men need to learn to stand firm, they retreat too easily, surrender too quickly, abandon what they should have held. But other men need to learn when to let go, they hold too tightly, refuse to adapt, confuse their preferences with God's purposes. Both errors are possible, and both are damaging.

How do you know the difference? Several questions help. Is God directing you to hold or to release? Have you sought counsel from trusted brothers who can see what you can't? Are you holding firm from faith or from fear? Is your perseverance producing fruit or just prolonging futility? Are you standing on conviction or on pride?

This is where the accountability we discussed in Chapter Eight becomes essential.

The man standing alone cannot easily distinguish perseverance from stubbornness, his own perspective is too limited. But the man in community has brothers who can speak truth, who can confirm when he should hold and confront when he should release. Accountability protects standing firm from becoming merely standing stuck.

Standing Firm Together

Standing firm is harder alone than in brotherhood. This has been true throughout the book's themes, and it's especially true here. The man trying to hold his ground without support will exhaust himself faster than the man reinforced by others.

During that season of accumulated pressure, the financial strain, the relational fracture, the health uncertainty, what kept me standing was not merely my own resolve but the brothers who stood with me. They prayed when I couldn't find words. They reminded me of truth when lies felt more real. They asked how I was actually doing and wouldn't accept the easy answer. They checked on me consistently, not just in the initial crisis but through the long months when the pressure continued.

This is the design. We were never meant to stand alone. When Paul describes the armor of God in Ephesians 6, he's not writing to individuals, he's writing to a community. The "you" who puts on the armor and stands firm is plural. It's the community standing together, each member's strength reinforcing the others, each member's faithfulness encouraging the rest.

Ecclesiastes captures this reality:

"Though one may be overpowered, two can defend themselves. A cord of three strands is not quickly broken." Ecclesiastes 4:12

One may be overpowered, alone, even the strong man eventually falls. But two can defend themselves, and three together become far stronger than the sum of their parts. If you're trying to stand firm alone, you're making it unnecessarily hard. Find the brothers who will stand with you. Let them reinforce your position. And be ready to do the same for them when their pressure arrives.

When You've Already Given Ground

Perhaps as you read this chapter, you're aware that you've already failed to stand firm. You've already retreated. You've already compromised. You've already given ground that you shouldn't have given. The question pressing on you isn't how to stand firm but whether recovery is possible after you've already fallen.

The answer is yes. Falling doesn't disqualify you from standing again. Giving ground doesn't mean you've permanently lost it. The discipline of standing firm includes the discipline of getting back up after you've been knocked down, and refusing to let past failure determine future faithfulness.

This is where the confession we discussed in Chapter Four becomes essential. Acknowledge what happened. Name the ground you gave, the compromise you made, the retreat you took. Bring it into the light with God and with trusted brothers. Confession clears the shame that would keep you down and opens the path to restoration.

Peter is the model here. He declared he would stand firm even if everyone else fell away. Then, when pressure came, he denied Jesus three times, a catastrophic failure to stand firm at the moment it mattered most. But Peter's story didn't end with his failure. Jesus restored him, recommissioned him, and Peter became the rock he had failed to be that night. His earlier failure didn't disqualify his later faithfulness.

If you've fallen, get up. If you've given ground, reclaim what you can and hold the line from where you are. If you've compromised, confess it and return to integrity. The discipline of standing firm isn't perfection, it's persistence. It's falling seven times and rising eight. It's refusing to let failure have the final word.

What Standing Firm Produces

The man who learns to stand firm becomes someone different, someone who can be trusted by God, by others, and by himself.

He becomes a man who can be trusted by God. God entrusts greater responsibility to men who've proven they won't crumble under pressure. The servant who stands firm with little is given more. The leader who holds his ground when tested is promoted to harder assignments. Standing firm is how you demonstrate the character that qualifies you for expanded influence.

He becomes a man others can follow. People don't follow the man who folds when things get difficult. They follow the man who holds his ground, the man they know won't abandon them when pressure arrives, won't compromise when it would be convenient, won't retreat when advancing gets costly. Authority flows from consistency under pressure, and standing firm is how that consistency is demonstrated.

He becomes a man who can trust himself. Every time you stand firm when you wanted to retreat, you build evidence that you're the man you hope to be. Every time you hold your ground when everything pushed against you, you develop confidence that you can do it again. Standing firm creates a track record you can draw on when future pressure arrives, proof that you've endured before and can endure again.

Paul described this result to the Corinthians:

"Therefore, my dear brothers and sisters, stand firm. Let nothing move you. Always give yourselves fully to the work of the Lord, because you know that your labor in the Lord is not in vain." 1 Corinthians 15:58

Stand firm. Let nothing move you. The labor is not in vain, even when you can't see the fruit, even when the results don't match the effort, even when the pressure makes you wonder if any of it matters. It matters. The standing firm itself matters, regardless of what it produces in visible results. And the man who stands firm discovers that he's become something through the standing that he couldn't have become any other way.

* * *

That season of accumulated pressure eventually passed. The financial situation stabilized through a combination of hard work and provision I hadn't expected. The fractured friendship, though never fully restored, found a place of peace. The health scare became managable rdespite its serious nature.

But what remained, what I carry with me still, is what I became through the standing. I'm not the same man who entered that season. I know now that I can endure more than I thought. I know that the anchor holds even when everything else gives way. I know that the discipline of standing firm, practiced through one impossible day after another, builds a strength that no amount of comfortable living ever could.

The arena doesn't require perfection. It requires persistence. It doesn't reward men who never get hit. It rewards men who never give their ground away, who take the pressure, feel the weight, and refuse to be moved.

So here's the question I want you to sit with:

Where is life currently pressuring you to retreat, and what would it look like to stand firm there instead?

Name the pressure. Identify what it's pushing you toward. Decide, now, before the pressure intensifies, that you won't be moved. Anchor yourself in something eternal. Get brothers around you who will stand with you. And when everything in you wants to run, choose instead to stand.

Stand firm. Let nothing move you. That's the discipline that separates the unstable from the grounded, the temporary from the lasting, the men who enter the arena from the men who stay there.

You don't need to be perfect. You just need to be planted. Stand firm, and you become the man the arena can't break.

CHAPTER THIRTEEN

Guarding Your Mind

"We demolish arguments and every pretension that sets itself up against the knowledge of God, and we take captive every thought to make it obedient to Christ."

2 Corinthians 10:5

* * *

The attack came at 3 a.m.

I woke from sleep with my mind already racing, not gradually coming to consciousness but instantly alert, flooded with thoughts that felt urgent and overwhelming. Every fear I had been managing during daylight hours surged forward in the darkness. Every worst-case scenario paraded through my imagination as if it were inevitable. Every voice of accusation and inadequacy spoke at once, and I had no defense against them.

For two hours I lay there, unable to sleep, unable to stop the spiral. One anxious thought connected to another, which triggered a memory of a past failure, which generated fear about a future outcome, which circled back to reinforce the original anxiety. My mind had become an echo chamber of fear, and I was trapped inside it.

By the time morning came, I was exhausted before my day had even begun. And this wasn't an isolated incident, it was becoming a pattern. Nights of racing thoughts followed by days of mental fog. Seasons where my mind felt like enemy territory, occupied by forces I couldn't seem to expel.

The turning point came when I realized I had been treating my thought life as something that happened to me rather than something I was responsible to steward. I was waiting passively for the mental attacks to stop rather than actively fighting them. I was hoping the anxious spirals would exhaust themselves rather than learning to interrupt them. I was a victim of my own mind because I had never learned to guard it.

What followed was one of the most important disciplines I've ever developed: the practice of taking every thought captive, of guarding the gates of my mind, of refusing to let lies set up residence unchallenged. It didn't happen overnight. It required learning new skills, building new patterns, and fighting battles I had previously surrendered by default. But the freedom that came from a guarded mind was worth every effort it required.

Your mind is the battlefield. Your thoughts are weapons, either for you or against you. And your attention is the territory everyone is trying to capture. If the enemy can get your mind, he doesn't need your body. If he can shape your thoughts, he doesn't need to touch your circumstances. If he can direct your attention, he can derail your purpose without you ever realizing what happened. Guarding your mind isn't optional for the man in the arena. It's survival.

Where Every Battle Begins

Your thoughts lead; your life follows. This is true whether you're paying attention to it or not. The man who thinks weak thoughts lives a weak life. The man who thinks fearful thoughts lives a fearful life. The man who thinks undisciplined thoughts lives an undisciplined life. Your external circumstances eventually conform to your internal patterns.

This is why the enemy attacks your mind first. He rarely begins with your circumstances, that would be too obvious, and you might recognize the attack and resist. Instead, he begins with your thoughts, whispering lies that sound like your own internal voice: You're not enough. You're failing. You're falling behind. You're alone. God isn't really with you. You should quit.

These attacks connect to what we explored in Chapter Five about fear, doubt, and comparison. Those enemies don't operate externally, they attack from within, through your thought life. Fear plants scenarios in your imagination. Doubt questions what you know to be true. Comparison whispers that others are succeeding while you're falling behind. The battlefield is your mind, and the weapons are the thoughts that either defend truth or advance lies.

Paul understood this when he described the nature of spiritual warfare:

"For though we live in the world, we do not wage war as the world does. The weapons we fight with are not the weapons of the world. On the contrary, they have divine power to demolish strongholds. We demolish arguments and every pretension that sets itself up against the knowledge of God, and we take captive every thought to make it obedient to Christ."
2 Corinthians 10:3-5

Notice what Paul says we're demolishing: strongholds, arguments, pretensions that set themselves up against the knowledge of God. These are mental structures, patterns of thinking that have established themselves in opposition to truth. And notice the response: we take captive every thought. Not some thoughts.

Not the obviously bad thoughts. Every thought, examined, evaluated, and made obedient to Christ.

This is active, not passive. You don't wait for thoughts to leave on their own. You take them captive. You exercise authority over what's allowed to remain in your mind. The man who won't do this work becomes a prisoner of whatever thoughts happen to show up, and the enemy will make sure destructive ones show up regularly.

How Lies Become Strongholds

A stronghold is a lie you've agreed with long enough that it feels like truth. It starts as an external thought, something whispered by the enemy, absorbed from culture, or adopted from painful experience. But when you agree with it, when you accept it as true rather than challenging it, it begins to take root. Over time, repeated agreement transforms the lie from something you hear into something you believe about yourself, about God, about reality.

This is how the stronghold of inadequacy forms. A young man fails at something important. The enemy whispers, "You're not enough." Instead of challenging the lie with truth, recognizing that failure doesn't define identity, that adequacy comes from Christ not performance, the young man agrees. He begins to believe the lie. And over years, "you're not enough" becomes so deeply embedded that it feels like fundamental truth about who he is. He can't even recognize it as a lie anymore because it's been there so long it seems like reality.

This is how the stronghold of fear forms. A man experiences something painful or frightening. The enemy whispers, "That will happen again. You need to protect yourself. Don't risk, don't trust, don't step out." Instead of challenging the lie, recognizing that God's presence provides courage, that fear is not from God, the man agrees. He begins to organize his life around avoiding the feared outcome. And over time, fear becomes his operating system, so deeply embedded he doesn't remember life without it.

Strongholds form through agreement and repetition. Every time you entertain a lie without challenging it, you strengthen its hold. Every time you agree with the accuser's whisper, you give it more authority in your mind. The thought that seemed intrusive at first becomes familiar, then normal, then foundational. What started as an attack becomes an identity.

This is why guarding your mind is so important. The time to address a lie is when it first arrives, before it's taken root, before you've agreed with it, before repetition has made it feel true. The longer you wait, the harder the stronghold is to demolish. Thoughts that are challenged immediately remain external attacks.

Thoughts that are tolerated become internal structures that require sustained effort to tear down.

Taking Thoughts Captive

"Take every thought captive" sounds good as a concept. But what does it actually look like in practice? How do you capture something as slippery and fast-moving as a thought?

The first step is recognition, noticing what's happening in your mind rather than being carried along by it unconsciously. Most destructive thought patterns operate below the level of awareness. You're anxious but don't notice the specific thoughts generating the anxiety. You're discouraged but don't identify the lies fueling the discouragement. The thought is doing its work while you're oblivious to its presence.

Practice stepping back from your thoughts and observing them. Ask yourself: What am I actually thinking right now? What specific words or images are running through my mind? This creates distance between you and the thought, you're no longer identified with it but examining it from outside. The thought that felt like truth when you were merged with it becomes visible as something that might or might not be true when you step back to examine it.

The second step is evaluation, testing the thought against truth. Is this thought consistent with what Scripture says? Is it consistent with God's character? Is it consistent with my identity in Christ? Many thoughts that feel urgent and true crumble under examination. The whisper "you're not enough" contradicts Paul's teaching that "I can do all things through Christ who strengthens me." The whisper "God has abandoned you" contradicts God's promise to never leave or forsake His people. The lie reveals itself as a lie when held up to truth.

The third step is replacement, actively substituting truth for the lie. It's not enough to reject the false thought; you must replace it with something true. This is what Paul taught the Philippians:

"Finally, brothers and sisters, whatever is true, whatever is noble, whatever is right, whatever is pure, whatever is lovely, whatever is admirable, if anything is excellent or praiseworthy, think about such things." Philippians 4:8

"Think about such things." Direct your mind intentionally toward what is true, noble, right, pure, lovely, admirable, excellent, praiseworthy. This isn't passive, it's active redirection of your attention from what's destructive to what's constructive. When the lie says "you're failing," you don't just reject the lie; you replace it with truth: "God's grace is sufficient, and His strength is made perfect in weakness." When fear says "you should quit," you replace it with "God has not given me a spirit of fear, but of power, love, and a sound mind."

This process, recognize, evaluate, replace, becomes more automatic with practice. At first it feels slow and deliberate, like learning any new skill. But over time, you develop the capacity to catch lies quickly, evaluate them against truth instinctively, and replace them before they take root. What required concentrated effort initially becomes a trained response.

Breaking the Spiral

Some mental patterns aren't single thoughts but spirals, one anxious thought triggering another, which triggers another, until you're caught in a cycle that feeds itself. The 3 a.m. attack I described earlier was this kind of spiral. Understanding how spirals work helps you break them.

Spirals build momentum through connection. One thought links to another, and each connection increases the emotional charge. You think about a financial concern, which connects to a fear about providing for your family, which connects to a memory of a past failure, which connects to a worry about your competence, which loops back to reinforce the original financial concern, now with much more emotional weight than it started with.

The key to breaking spirals is interruption. You have to disrupt the chain before it builds unstoppable momentum. Several practices help with this.

Physical interruption can break mental spirals. Get up and move. Walk outside. Do something with your hands. The physical change can disrupt the mental pattern, giving you space to reset. Your body and mind are connected; changing what your body is doing can change what your mind is doing.

Verbal interruption can break spirals. Speak truth out loud, even if you're alone, even if it feels strange. There's something about voicing truth that has more power than merely thinking it. When the spiral is running, say out loud: "God is faithful. His grace is sufficient. I am not alone. This fear is not from God." The spoken word interrupts the internal chatter.

Gratitude interruption can break spirals. Force your mind to name specific things you're grateful for. The spiral runs on fear and negativity; gratitude introduces a different substance that the spiral cannot incorporate. You cannot be simultaneously grateful and anxious about the same thing. Gratitude doesn't solve the concern, but it breaks the spiral so you can address the concern from a stable place.

Scripture interruption is the most powerful. Have specific verses ready for specific attacks. When fear spirals, speak 2 Timothy 1:7: "God has not given us a spirit of fear, but of power, love, and a sound mind." When inadequacy spirals, speak 2 Corinthians 12:9: "My grace is sufficient for you, for my power is made perfect in weakness." When condemnation spirals, speak Romans 8:1: "There is now no condemnation for those who are in Christ Jesus." The truth of God's Word has power to break what your own thoughts cannot.

Guarding the Gates

Your mind is shaped by what you give it. This is why guarding your mind isn't just about managing thoughts that arise, it's about controlling what you allow to enter in the first place.

Consider what you're consuming. What do you watch? What do you read? What do you scroll through? What voices do you listen to regularly? What enters your mind through your entertainment, your social media, your news intake? Every input is either building something constructive or depositing something destructive. There is no neutral consumption.

If you constantly consume anxiety, news designed to alarm, content designed to outrage, feeds designed to trigger comparison, don't be surprised when your mind is anxious. If you consume chaos, fragmented attention, endless scrolling, constant notification, don't be surprised when your mind can't focus. If you consume content that degrades your values, entertainment that celebrates what you know is wrong, don't be surprised when your convictions weaken.

You cannot expect clarity from a mind filled with clutter. You cannot expect peace from a mind fed anxiety. You cannot expect purity from a mind consuming corruption. Your mental diet is as important as your spiritual one, and often they're the same thing.

This is where the discipline of saying no from Chapter Eleven applies to your inputs, not just your commitments. You have to develop a filter, criteria that determine what gets access to your mind and what doesn't. Does this strengthen my spirit or weaken it? Does this align with truth or contradict it? Does this build my faith or undermine it? Does this protect my peace or assault it? Does this move me toward wisdom or away from it? If the answer is negative, it doesn't belong in your mind regardless of how entertaining it is, regardless of how everyone else is consuming it.

Equally important is what you proactively feed your mind. It's not enough to eliminate the negative; you must cultivate the positive. Scripture, regularly, substantively, not as brief devotional snippets but as sustained engagement with God's Word. Prayer, not just talking but listening, creating space for God's voice.

Silence, time without input, where your mind can settle and your soul can hear. Worthy content, books, teaching, and conversations that build rather than deplete.

The man who guards his inputs has a much easier time guarding his thoughts.

The battle against destructive thinking is far simpler when you're not constantly introducing destructive material through unguarded gates.

The Power of Silence

Noise destroys clarity. Most men live in constant noise, the background hum of media, the endless stream of notifications, the perpetual presence of some form of input. This noise isn't just external; it creates internal noise that makes clear thinking nearly impossible.

Most people don't hear God not because He's silent but because their life is loud. The still, small voice doesn't compete with the shouting. The gentle whisper of the Spirit gets drowned by the constant chatter. If you want to guard your mind, you need silence, regular, intentional, protected space where there's no input, no stimulation, no noise.

Silence does several things that noise cannot. It sharpens discernment, in silence you begin to notice thoughts you'd otherwise miss, distinguish between your voice and other voices, hear what's been covered by the noise. It restores peace, the constant stimulation of noise creates a baseline of agitation that silence allows to settle. It resets perspective, when you step out of the noise, you often discover that things that seemed urgent weren't, that anxieties that seemed overwhelming shrink when examined in quiet.

This is why the spiritual disciplines include solitude and silence, not as punishment but as restoration. Jesus regularly withdrew to quiet places to pray. The psalmist wrote, "Be still, and know that I am God." The invitation to silence is an invitation to a different kind of knowing, a deeper kind of hearing, a clearer kind of seeing.

Building silence into your life requires intention. It won't happen by accident in a world designed to fill every moment with noise. You have to create it, turn off the podcast during the commute sometimes, put the phone in another room during morning prayer, protect time where there's simply no input. The discomfort you feel in silence reveals how dependent you've become on noise, and that discomfort is precisely why you need the silence.

When the Battle Needs Reinforcement

Everything in this chapter assumes a normal range of mental struggle, the kind of thought battles that every person faces, the kind of anxiety that responds to spiritual discipline, the kind of patterns that can be changed through the practices described. But some mental health challenges require more than spiritual discipline alone.

Recognizing this isn't weakness; it's wisdom.

Clinical anxiety, depression, trauma responses, and other conditions often have biological and psychological components that spiritual practices alone don't fully address. The man who breaks his leg doesn't refuse medical treatment because he should be able to pray through it. Similarly, the man whose brain chemistry is contributing to his mental struggle shouldn't refuse appropriate professional help because he thinks he should be able to discipline his way through it.

If your mental battles are persistent and severe, if they're significantly impairing your daily functioning, if they're not responding to the practices that help others, if they're accompanied by thoughts of self-harm, seeking professional support isn't failure. It's stewardship of the mind God gave you. A counselor, a therapist, a doctor, these can be part of how God provides help, just as He provides healing through medical professionals for physical conditions.

This isn't either/or, spiritual discipline or professional help. For many people, it's both/and. The spiritual practices of guarding your mind remain valuable alongside whatever professional support you need.

Scripture still speaks truth. Prayer still provides alignment. Silence still offers clarity. These work in concert with appropriate treatment, not as a replacement for it.

The enemy would love for you to suffer in silence, convinced that asking for help is shameful. But the man who recognizes his need and seeks appropriate support is stronger than the man who refuses help out of pride. Guard your mind by whatever means are appropriate, including the humility to get help when you need it.

* * *

Those 3 a.m. attacks haven't disappeared entirely. The enemy still probes for weakness, still whispers lies, still looks for unguarded moments to exploit. But the battle looks different now than it did before I learned to guard my mind.

Now when the spiral begins, I recognize it. I've learned to step back and observe rather than being swept along unconsciously. Now when lies whisper, I have truth ready, specific verses memorized for specific attacks. Now when anxiety builds momentum, I have interruption strategies that work: speaking truth aloud, moving physically, naming gratitude, engaging Scripture. The battle is still real, but I'm no longer a passive victim. I'm an active combatant in the war for my own mind.

A guarded mind is a dangerous mind, dangerous to darkness. The man whose thoughts are captured by truth can't be manipulated by lies. The man whose mind is anchored in Scripture can't be destabilized by circumstances. The man who has learned to interrupt the enemy's spirals can't be paralyzed by the enemy's attacks. He becomes steady, focused, spiritually awake, prepared for whatever the arena brings.

So here's the question I want you to sit with:

What thoughts have you been tolerating that you should have been taking captive, and what truth needs to replace them?

You probably already know. There's a lie that's been running unchallenged. There's a spiral that's been allowed to spin. There's a thought pattern that's been tolerated so long it feels like truth. Name it. Recognize it for what it is. Evaluate it against Scripture. And replace it with the truth that sets free.

Guard your mind. Take every thought captive. And become the man whose mind is so well-defended that the enemy has to look elsewhere for easier targets.

The arena tests your mind before it tests anything else. Guard it well.

CHAPTER FOURTEEN

Facing Temptation

"No temptation has overtaken you except what is common to mankind. And God is faithful; he will not let you be tempted beyond what you can bear. But when you are tempted, he will also provide a way out so that you can endure it."

1 Corinthians 10:13

* * *

The temptation didn't arrive as danger. It arrived as relief.

I was exhausted, weeks of pressure without adequate rest, running on fumes, carrying burdens I should have been sharing but was handling alone. The thing that tempted me didn't announce itself as something that could damage my life. It presented itself as something I deserved, something that would take the edge off, something that wasn't really that bad. Just a small comfort. Just this once. Just to get through this difficult season.

The rationalizations came easily because I was too depleted to think clearly.

You've been working so hard. You're under more pressure than most people understand. No one would blame you. No one will know. You can course-correct later. The logic felt airtight in the moment, and I gave in.

What followed wasn't the relief that was promised. It was shame, the immediate, crushing awareness that I had traded something real for something empty. The momentary comfort evaporated, leaving behind the weight of compromise. I knew I had lost something: not just my streak of resistance but my clarity, my confidence, my sense of walking in integrity with God. The thing that had promised relief delivered regret.

That experience, and the painful process of confession, repentance, and rebuilding that followed, taught me more about temptation than years of successfully avoiding it had. I learned that temptation is most dangerous when you're depleted, that it always presents itself as reasonable, that it promises comfort but delivers consequences. I learned that secrecy fertilizes sin, that isolation makes resistance impossible, and that the moment of temptation is not where the battle is primarily won or lost. I learned that falling is not final, but it is costly, and that understanding how temptation actually works is essential for any man serious about living in the arena.

How Temptation Actually Works

Temptation doesn't show up dressed like danger. It shows up dressed like relief, comfort, escape, validation, attention, pleasure, distraction. If temptation announced itself honestly, "this will damage your integrity, harm your relationships, and leave you full of regret", no one would fall. It works precisely because it appears beneficial in the moment, offering something that seems good while hiding the cost.

James describes the progression with disturbing clarity:

"Each person is tempted when they are dragged away by their own desire and enticed. Then, after desire has conceived, it gives birth to sin; and sin, when it is full-grown, gives birth to death." James 1:14-15

Notice the sequence: desire, enticement, conception, birth of sin, death.

Temptation exploits existing desires, which aren't sinful in themselves, and entices them toward wrong objects or wrong timing. The desire for comfort becomes the enticement toward compromise. The desire for validation becomes the enticement toward approval-seeking that abandons conviction. The desire for pleasure becomes the enticement toward pleasure obtained wrongly. Temptation doesn't create desire; it hijacks it.

Understanding this sequence shows where intervention is most effective. Once desire has conceived and given birth to sin, you're in damage control. But earlier in the sequence, when desire is being enticed but hasn't yet conceived, you have far more leverage. The battle against temptation is most easily won in the early stages, nefore momentum has built, before rationalization has set in, before the pull has become overwhelming.

Temptation also targets specific conditions. It rarely hits you when you're strong, rested, connected, and spiritually alert. It hits you when you're depleted, discouraged, isolated, stressed, frustrated, or overlooked. The enemy waits for vulnerability. He aims for your weak moments, not your strong ones. This is why managing your condition, rest, connection, spiritual health, is itself a form of fighting temptation.

The man who lets himself become depleted and isolated has already positioned himself to fall.

The Lies Temptation Tells

Temptation speaks in rationalizations that sound reasonable in the moment but reveal themselves as lies in the aftermath. Recognizing these lies before you believe them is essential to resistance.

"You deserve this." Temptation often frames compromise as reward, something you've earned through your hard work, your suffering, your faithfulness in other areas. This lie ignores that obedience isn't a credit system where good behavior in one area earns permission for compromise in another. What you actually deserve is the fruit of obedience; what temptation offers is a counterfeit that steals that fruit.

"Just this once." Temptation minimizes by isolating the decision from its pattern. This one time won't matter. But every compromise makes the next one easier. Every "just this once" weakens resistance for the next time. Sin has momentum; giving in once makes giving in again more likely. The exception wants to become the rule.

"No one will know." Temptation exploits the illusion of secrecy. If no one sees, it doesn't count. But God sees. You know. And the hidden compromise changes you even if no human witnesses it. The man who hides his sin becomes a man who lives divided, one version for public consumption, another in secret. That division corrodes everything.

"You can repent later." Temptation offers presumption disguised as grace. Yes, forgiveness is available, but counting on future forgiveness while choosing present sin treats grace as license. Paul addressed this directly: "Shall we go on sinning so that grace may increase? By no means!" The man who plans to repent later reveals that he doesn't actually understand what repentance means.

"It's not that bad." Temptation minimizes the sin by comparing it to worse alternatives. At least you're not doing what that guy is doing. At least it's not the really serious stuff. This lie ignores that all sin, whether culturally acceptable or scandalous, separates you from God and damages your soul. The question isn't whether others have done worse; it's whether this is obedience or compromise.

When you hear these voices, recognize them for what they are: lies from an enemy who wants your destruction and knows how to make destruction look reasonable. The moment you're rationalizing is the moment to be most suspicious of your own reasoning.

How Jesus Faced Temptation

Jesus was tempted, not theoretically but actually, in ways that were real and intense. The writer of Hebrews emphasizes this:

"For we do not have a high priest who is unable to empathize with our weaknesses, but we have one who has been tempted in every way, just as we are, yet he did not sin." Hebrews 4:15

"Tempted in every way, just as we are." This isn't Jesus observing temptation from a safe distance; it's Jesus experiencing what we experience. He knows the pull. He understands the pressure. And how He handled temptation provides a model for how we can handle it.

Consider Jesus' temptation in the wilderness. He had been fasting for forty days, physically depleted, alone, in the wilderness. The enemy chose this moment to attack, exploiting vulnerability just as he does with us. And the temptations he offered were sophisticated, each one appealing to legitimate desires while proposing illegitimate means.

"Turn these stones into bread." The desire to eat after forty days wasn't sinful; it was human. The temptation was to use His power to serve His appetites apart from the Father's direction. Jesus responded: "Man shall not live on bread alone, but on every word that comes from the mouth of God." He met the temptation with Scripture, grounding His response in truth rather than negotiating with desire.

"Throw yourself down; the angels will catch you." The temptation to prove His identity, to force God's hand, to test whether God would really protect Him. Jesus responded: "Do not put the Lord your God to the test." Again, Scripture, specific truth applied to the specific temptation.

"Worship me and I'll give you all the kingdoms." The offer of a shortcut to what Jesus came to accomplish, authority over nations, but obtained through compromise rather than the cross. Jesus responded: "Worship the Lord your God, and serve him only." Scripture again, and the encounter ended. The devil left until a more opportune time.

Three things stand out in how Jesus faced temptation. First, He used Scripture, not vague spiritual thoughts but specific texts applied to specific attacks. The Word of God was His weapon. Second, He didn't engage in extended dialogue with the tempter. He didn't negotiate, didn't consider the offers carefully, didn't weigh pros and cons. He responded with truth and moved on. Third, He was spiritually prepared before the temptation arrived. His relationship with the Father was intact; His identity was clear; He knew who He was and what He came to do. The temptation couldn't confuse someone with that kind of clarity.

What to Do in the Moment

When temptation arrives, you need more than principles, you need practices. Here's what actually helps in the moment of pull.

First, slow down. Speed is temptation's ally. When you're moving fast, reacting rather than responding, you don't have space to think clearly. Create a gap between stimulus and response. Take a breath. Step back mentally before you act physically. Most temptations lose power when you pause long enough to see them clearly rather than being swept along in the momentum.

Second, name what's happening. Say it, out loud if possible, internally at minimum: "This is temptation. The enemy is attacking me right now. This is not what it appears to be." Naming temptation externally diminishes its power. As long as it operates unnamed in the shadows of your mind, it has leverage. When you drag it into the light and label it accurately, something shifts.

Third, recall the cost. Temptation shows you the pleasure; force yourself to see the aftermath. Remember what the last compromise cost you, the shame, the regret, the lost confidence, the damaged trust. Project forward: If I give in, how will I feel in an hour? Tomorrow? What will I have lost? The momentary pleasure rarely survives this kind of honest projection.

Fourth, use Scripture as a weapon, like Jesus did. Have specific verses ready for your specific temptations. When lust attacks, have a verse ready. When anger attacks, have a verse ready. When the temptation to quit attacks, have a verse ready. Speak the verse out loud. Truth has power, especially spoken truth, especially truth from God's Word.

Fifth, remove yourself from the situation when possible. Sometimes the most effective thing is simply to leave, change your physical location, close the browser, put down the phone, walk away from the conversation. You're not being weak by fleeing; you're being wise. Paul told Timothy to flee youthful lusts, not to stand and fight them toe-to-toe. Some battles are won by strategic withdrawal.

Sixth, call someone. The temptation that thrives in isolation weakens when exposed. Text a brother: "I'm being tempted right now. Pray for me." The act of confession, even brief confession in the moment, breaks something. You're no longer alone in the fight. The light has entered. And often, by the time you've finished the conversation, the pull has weakened.

God promises to provide a way of escape with every temptation. These practices are often what the escape route looks like. The question is whether you'll look for it and take it.

Winning Before the Moment Arrives

The battle against temptation is most easily won before the temptation arrives. The decisions you make when you're not tempted determine your capacity to resist when you are.

Build habits that keep you strong. This connects directly to Chapter Seven. The man with consistent spiritual habits, Scripture, prayer, Sabbath, is harder to tempt than the man who has let those habits slip. The man who is rested and connected is harder to tempt than the man who is depleted and isolated. Your daily disciplines are not just good practices; they're protective armor against the attacks that will come.

Set boundaries before you need them. Decide in advance what you will and won't do, where you will and won't go, what you will and won't consume. These decisions are much easier to make when you're thinking clearly than when you're in the grip of temptation. A boundary established in a clear moment protects you in a murky one.

Guard your inputs. What you consume shapes what you desire. The man who constantly consumes content that inflames wrong desires is making future temptation harder to resist. The man who guards what enters his mind, as we discussed in Chapter Thirteen, is building resistance before the attack even comes.

Stay accountable. This connects to Chapter Eight. The man who has brothers asking hard questions regularly is less likely to fall than the man who answers to no one. The temptation that thrives in secrecy withers under consistent accountability. If you know someone will ask about it, you're more likely to resist.

Know your patterns. When are you most vulnerable? What conditions precede your temptation? What triggers set you up to fall? Understanding your patterns helps you recognize danger before you're in it and take protective action while you still have clarity. The man who knows his vulnerabilities can guard them; the man who doesn't will be surprised again and again.

Know your identity. This connects to Chapter Two. When you know who you are, whose you are, what you're called to, temptation loses leverage. "I am not that man anymore" is armor. "I am not ruled by this" is a weapon. "I am a man who obeys God first" is a declaration that reframes the temptation from an invitation to be considered to an attack to be repelled. Identity clarity is one of the strongest defenses you have.

When You Fall

Perhaps you're reading this chapter not in preparation for future temptation but in the aftermath of recent failure. You fell. You gave in. You compromised. And now you're wondering what to do, whether recovery is possible, whether you've disqualified yourself, whether there's a way back.

There is. Falling is not final. The enemy would love for you to believe that one failure ends the fight, that you might as well keep falling since you've already fallen, that there's no point in getting back up. These are lies, just like the lies that led you to fall in the first place.

The path back begins with confession, to God and to trusted brothers. This connects to everything we explored in Chapter Four. The sin you hide becomes the sin that owns you. Bringing it into the light, painful as that is, breaks its power.

Confession isn't punishment; it's the pathway to freedom.

After confession comes repentance, not just feeling sorry but actually turning. Repentance means changing direction, addressing the conditions that led to the fall, building structures that prevent the same failure. Repentance without change is just regret; genuine repentance produces observable difference.

After repentance comes restoration, receiving grace and rebuilding trust.

God's forgiveness is immediate upon genuine repentance; trust with others may take longer to rebuild. That's appropriate. Grace doesn't eliminate consequences, and restored relationship with God doesn't automatically mean restored credibility with people. Accept that rebuilding takes time, and do the patient work of demonstrating change.

The fall also provides information. What led to it? What conditions made you vulnerable? What boundaries failed? What accountability was missing? Your failure, examined honestly, teaches you something about your weaknesses and gaps. The man who falls and learns falls less often than the man who falls and merely feels bad.

Finally, guard against false guilt that keeps you down after God has lifted you.

The enemy accuses after you've fallen, trying to keep you in shame after God has granted forgiveness. If you've genuinely confessed and repented, the ongoing condemnation isn't from God, it's from the accuser. Receive grace and get back in the fight.

The Temptation You Defeat Changes You

Temptation faced and defeated is not just a threat survived, it's a formation experience. Every temptation you resist becomes a strengthening of your discipline, a deepening of your character, a testimony that you can draw on when future temptation arrives.

The first time you resist a particular temptation is the hardest. The pull is strong, the outcome uncertain, the resistance requiring everything you have. But once you've resisted once, something shifts. You know you can do it because you've done it. The second resistance is slightly easier. The third easier still. Over time, what was once a fierce battle becomes almost automatic, the temptation still exists, but it no longer has the power it once had.

This is how self-mastery develops. A man who cannot master himself cannot master anything else. Temptation is the test that reveals whether you lead your desires or your desires lead you. Every victory trains you for the next battle. Every time you choose obedience over impulse, you're building the capacity for future obedience.

The arena rewards self-mastery. The man who has learned to face temptation without falling becomes someone God can trust with greater responsibility. If you can be trusted with your desires, you can be trusted with influence. If you can lead yourself, you can lead others. If you can resist when no one is watching, you have the character that public leadership requires.

Temptation is not a sign of weakness. It's the battleground where strong men are formed.

* * *

That failure I described at the beginning of this chapter, the one that came when I was depleted and rationalized my way into compromise, was painful. The confession was hard. The rebuilding was slow. I wish I had never fallen.

But I learned things through that failure that success couldn't have taught me.

I learned that I'm vulnerable in ways I hadn't wanted to admit. I learned that isolation and depletion set me up to fall. I learned that the rationalizations that sound reasonable in the moment reveal themselves as lies in the aftermath. And I learned that grace is real, that falling doesn't have to be final, that the way back is difficult but possible, that God restores those who return to Him.

I also learned to fight differently. Now I know the warning signs. Now I have practices that work when the pull arrives. Now I have brothers who know my patterns and ask the hard questions. Now I understand that the battle is won primarily before the temptation arrives, in the habits, boundaries, accountability, and identity work that make resistance possible.

So here's the question I want you to sit with:

Where are you most vulnerable to temptation right now, and what preparation could you put in place before the next attack arrives?

You probably know your weakness. You've probably fallen to it before. The question is whether you'll keep fighting the same battle with the same inadequate defenses, or whether you'll build the habits, boundaries, accountability, and identity clarity that give you a chance to win.

Face the temptation. Fight it with everything you have and everything God provides. And become the man who has learned to stand where others fall.

The arena respects men who discipline their desires instead of being ruled by them. Join their ranks.

CHAPTER FIFTEEN

Emotional Control

"Better a patient person than a warrior, one with self-control than one who takes a city."

Proverbs 16:32

* * *

The words were out of my mouth before I could stop them.

I was frustrated, legitimately frustrated, responding to a situation that warranted some frustration. But the intensity of my response had nothing to do with the situation's actual severity. Something in me ignited, and before I had consciously decided to speak, I had already said things I couldn't take back. The look on my mother's face told me immediately what I had done. I had let my emotions drive, and now there was damage.

What followed was familiar: the slow realization that my reaction had been disproportionate to the trigger, the recognition that I had wounded someone I loved, the awkward attempt to apologize while also explaining what I had actually meant, as if explanation could undo impact. I had been here before. This wasn't new. The pattern was becoming undeniable: something would trigger me, emotion would surge, I would react before thinking, and then I would spend far longer cleaning up the damage than the original situation would have required to address calmly.

That incident, and the honest conversation with my mother that followed, began a season of serious work on emotional control. I had to admit something I had been avoiding: my emotions were real and they mattered, but I had been letting them lead in moments when I should have been leading them. The feeling was legitimate; the reaction it drove was not. And the people around me, the people I loved most, were paying the price for my lack of internal discipline.

What I learned in the months that followed transformed not just my family but my leadership, my friendships, and my walk with God. Emotional control isn't about suppressing feelings, that's numbness, and numbness is its own form of dysfunction. Emotional control is about mastering feelings: experiencing them fully, understanding what they're telling you, and choosing your response rather than letting the emotion choose for you. Strong men feel deeply. Strong men don't get ruled by what they feel. Learning the difference changed everything.

What Reactivity Actually Costs

Unchecked emotions always create collateral damage. One reactive moment can undo months of trust-building. One explosion can change how your children see you. One uncontrolled response can alter the trajectory of a relationship or opportunity.

The cost of emotional instability is always higher than it appears in the moment, because in the moment, you're only seeing the trigger, not the ripple effects of your reaction.

Proverbs captures this with striking imagery:

"Like a city whose walls are broken through is a person who lacks self-control."
Proverbs 25:28

A city with broken walls is defenseless. Whatever enemy wants to enter can enter. Whatever force wants to plunder can plunder. The city may have strong buildings inside, valuable resources, even capable people, but without walls, all of that is exposed to destruction. The man who lacks self-control is the same: whatever external pressure comes, it walks right in. Whatever trigger presents itself gains immediate access to his core. He has no buffer between stimulus and response, no protection between what he feels and what he does.

This connects directly to leadership. You cannot lead others well if you cannot lead yourself. If you can't discipline your reactions, your impulses, your frustration, your anger, your fear, your insecurity, then the people around you will pay for your lack of control. They'll learn to walk on eggshells around you. They'll hesitate to bring you bad news because they can't predict how you'll respond. They'll distance themselves emotionally because your instability makes closeness unsafe. Leadership requires emotional maturity; without it, your leadership becomes a liability rather than an asset.

Consider what's at stake: your marriage, where your spouse needs to experience you as safe and stable. Your parenting, where your children are learning emotional patterns from watching you. Your leadership, where people will only follow as far as they trust you. Your witness, where the world watches whether your faith produces different fruit than their lives do. In every domain, emotional reactivity undermines what you're trying to build.

Indicators, Not Commanders

Understanding what emotions actually are helps you relate to them properly. Emotions are indicators, they tell you that something is happening that matters to you. Anger indicates that something feels unjust or threatening. Fear indicates that something feels dangerous. Sadness indicates that something has been lost. Joy indicates that something good is present. Each emotion is information about your internal state and your perception of your circumstances.

But here's what emotions are not: they're not commanders. They provide information, not instructions. The feeling of anger tells you that something feels unjust; it doesn't tell you to explode, to attack, to say something cutting. The feeling of fear tells you that something feels dangerous; it doesn't tell you to retreat, to hide, to abandon your calling. The emotion provides data about your internal state; you decide what to do with that data.

Confusion happens when you treat emotions as truth rather than signals. The anger feels so intense that it seems to demand expression. The fear feels so real that it seems to require obedience. But intensity doesn't equal accuracy. Your emotions might be responding to something real, or they might be responding to a misperception, an old wound, a distorted interpretation. The emotion itself can't tell you which, it just reports how you feel, not whether that feeling is an accurate response to reality.

Emotional control begins when you learn to separate the feeling from the decision. The feeling is information; the decision is separate. You can acknowledge the anger without obeying it. You can recognize the fear without letting it direct your behavior. You can experience the sadness without being consumed by it. The emotion has permission to exist; it doesn't have permission to rule.

James understood this when he wrote:

"My dear brothers and sisters, take note of this: Everyone should be quick to listen, slow to speak and slow to become angry, because human anger does not produce the righteousness that God desires."
James 1:19-20

Slow to speak. Slow to become angry. Not because the emotion isn't real, it is.

Not because the situation doesn't matter, it might. But because the response requires more than just the feeling. It requires thought. It requires wisdom. It requires the pause that separates reaction from response.

Control Is Not Suppression

I need to say this clearly because many men misunderstand it: emotional control is not emotional suppression. You're not being called to be numb. You're not being called to disconnect from what you feel. You're not being called to pretend emotions don't exist or don't matter. That's not control, that's avoidance, and it produces its own damage.

Men who suppress emotions don't eliminate them; they bury them. And buried emotions don't stay buried, they leak out sideways in irritability, in passive aggression, in sudden explosions that seem to come from nowhere but actually come from years of unprocessed feeling. Suppression also creates distance in relationships; the man who can't access his own emotions can't connect deeply with others who are experiencing theirs. His spouse feels unknown. His children feel unseen. His friends experience him as unreachable.

Emotional control is something different. It means experiencing the emotion fully, feeling it, naming it, understanding what it's telling you, while maintaining the capacity to choose your response. You're not pretending the anger doesn't exist; you're feeling the anger while deciding how to address what triggered it. You're not pretending the fear is absent; you're acknowledging the fear while refusing to let it dictate your behavior. The emotion is present and honored; it just isn't in charge.

The fruit of the Spirit includes self-control:

"But the fruit of the Spirit is love, joy, peace, forbearance, kindness, goodness, faithfulness, gentleness and self-control."
Galatians 5:22-23

Self-control is fruit, something produced by the Spirit's work in you. It's listed alongside love, joy, peace, kindness, not as a contradiction of emotion but as its complement. The Spirit-filled life is not emotionless; it's emotionally mature. You experience love deeply. You experience joy fully. You experience peace genuinely.

And you exercise self-control consistently. All of these together, not some against others.

Building Awareness

You can't master what you refuse to notice. Emotional control begins with emotional awareness, the capacity to recognize what you're feeling, name it accurately, and understand what's driving it. For many men, this awareness is underdeveloped. They know they feel "bad" but can't distinguish between anger, sadness, fear, and frustration. They know something's wrong but can't identify the trigger. This vagueness makes control impossible; you can't manage what you can't see clearly.

Developing awareness requires asking honest questions. What am I actually feeling right now? Not what should I be feeling or what would be acceptable to feel, what am I actually feeling? Give it a specific name. Anger is different from frustration is different from disappointment is different from hurt. The more precisely you can name the emotion, the better you can understand it and respond to it.

Ask also what triggered this feeling. Something happened, external or internal, that activated this emotional response. What was it? Sometimes the trigger is obvious: someone said something cutting, something went wrong, a fear was realized. Sometimes the trigger is less obvious: something reminded you of an old wound, something threatened an insecurity you carry, something touched a belief you hold about yourself.

Ask what lies beneath the surface. Often the presenting emotion is sitting on top of something deeper. The anger might be covering fear. The frustration might be rooted in unmet expectation. The irritability might be exhaustion or loneliness or spiritual dryness. When you dig beneath the surface, you often find something more fundamental that the presenting emotion was trying to signal.

Pay attention to patterns. Your emotional reactions are probably not random, they follow patterns shaped by your history, your wounds, your beliefs about yourself and others. When do you tend to get triggered? What kinds of situations produce the strongest reactions? What themes keep showing up?

Understanding your patterns gives you the ability to anticipate triggers and prepare for them rather than being ambushed by them repeatedly.

This awareness work connects to Chapter Thirteen's discussion of guarding your mind. The thoughts running through your head are generating the emotions you feel. When you identify the thought,"they don't respect me," "I'm failing," "this is going to fall apart" you can evaluate whether the thought is true and address it before it produces an emotional reaction you can't control.

Regulating in the Moment

When emotion surges, you need more than principles, you need practices. Here's what actually helps when you feel yourself being pulled toward reactive behavior.

Create space between stimulus and response. This is the fundamental discipline. Something triggers you; before you react, you insert a pause. The pause can be brief, a deep breath, a count to ten, a moment of silence before speaking, but it's essential. Most emotional damage happens because a man reacted before he thought. The pause gives you time to think. It interrupts the automatic pathway from trigger to reaction and creates space for a chosen response.

Use your body to regulate your mind. Emotions are physical experiences, they show up in your body as much as your mind. Your heart rate increases. Your muscles tense. Your breathing shallows. These physical changes reinforce the emotional state, creating a feedback loop. But you can interrupt the loop from the body side. Slow your breathing deliberately. Relax your shoulders and jaw. Change your posture. Go

for a walk. These physical changes send signals to your brain that help regulate the emotional state.

Speak truth to yourself. In the moment of emotional surge, lies often drive the intensity: this is catastrophic, I can't handle this, they're attacking me, everything is falling apart. Combat these lies with truth, spoken truth if possible, internal truth at minimum. God is with me. This moment is not the whole story. I can respond rather than react. The truth won't eliminate the emotion, but it will moderate the intensity and create space for a measured response.

Remove yourself when necessary. Sometimes the wisest thing is to step away.

You recognize that you're not in a state to respond constructively, so you excuse yourself, take a walk, get some space before re-engaging. This isn't running away, it's strategic withdrawal. You'll return when you're regulated and able to address the situation from a grounded place rather than a reactive one.

Express the emotion appropriately rather than suppressing it. If you're angry, you can say "I'm feeling angry about this" without exploding. If you're hurt, you can express the hurt without attacking. Appropriate expression acknowledges the emotion without letting it drive destructive behavior. The feeling is named and communicated; it just doesn't take the wheel.

Building Long-Term Capacity

Emotional control is not primarily built in the moment of crisis, it's built in the daily rhythms that keep you regulated before crisis arrives.

This connects to Chapter Seven's emphasis on habits: the daily disciplines create the capacity you draw on when pressure comes.

Prayer keeps you spiritually regulated. Regular time with God aligns your perspective, reminds you of truth, and settles your soul. The man who prays consistently has a different baseline than the man who doesn't. He's more grounded going into challenging situations, more aware of God's presence when pressure arrives, more able to access spiritual resources in the moment.

Scripture renews your mind. The truth you internalize becomes available when you need it. The man who has been saturating his mind in Scripture has truth ready when lies try to drive emotional reaction. As we discussed in Chapter Thirteen, the mind filled with truth is harder to destabilize than the mind filled with whatever happened to enter.

Rest protects your capacity. Exhaustion depletes emotional resources. When you're running on empty, your ability to regulate collapses. You react to things that wouldn't have triggered you when rested. You lack the energy to create space between stimulus and response. Sleep, Sabbath, margin, these aren't luxuries; they're protection for your emotional capacity.

Physical exercise provides outlet and regulation. Your body is designed to move, and movement helps process emotion. The frustration that builds up has somewhere to go. The anxiety that accumulates gets discharged. Regular physical activity is one of the most effective emotional regulation practices available, not as a substitute for spiritual disciplines but alongside them.

Silence and solitude create space for self-awareness. In the noise of constant activity, you don't have room to notice what's happening internally. Regular time in quiet allows you to process what you've been experiencing, identify what's building, and address things before they erupt. The man who never gets quiet is often the man most surprised by his own emotional reactions, because he never had space to see them coming.

Breaking Emotional Agreements

Many emotional reactions don't originate in the present moment, they come from agreements you've unconsciously made over years, often rooted in old wounds, messages you absorbed, or conclusions you drew from painful experiences.

These agreements function like hidden programs running in the background. "I always mess things up." "No one really sees me." "I'm not good enough." "People always leave." "I have to protect myself because no one else will." Each agreement shapes how you interpret present situations and what emotions get triggered. The criticism from your boss doesn't just land as criticism, it activates the old agreement that you're not good enough, and suddenly you're reacting not just to what was said but to years of accumulated evidence that seems to confirm the agreement.

Breaking these agreements requires first identifying them. What conclusions about yourself do you carry? What do you believe about how people will treat you? What stories do you tell yourself about your own worth, your future, your relationships? These aren't always conscious; you may need to work backward from your reactions. When you have a disproportionate emotional response, ask what old agreement the situation is activating.

Once identified, agreements can be broken and replaced. This connects to the confession work from Chapter Four and the identity work from Chapter Two. You confess the lie you've been believing. You renounce it, actively, verbally, intentionally. And you replace it with truth: "I am not defined by my failures." "I am seen by God." "My worth comes from Christ, not from performance." "God will never leave me." "I am held by One stronger than my need to protect myself."

This replacement isn't a one-time event but an ongoing practice. The old agreements have been reinforced for years; the new truth needs repetition to take root. Every time the old agreement tries to activate, you replace it with the new truth. Over time, the emotional charge diminishes as the agreement loses its grip.

What Emotional Maturity Produces

A man who develops emotional control becomes a different kind of presence, in his family, in his leadership, in every environment he enters.

He becomes safe. The people around him don't have to walk on eggshells, wondering what version of him will show up. They can bring him difficult information without fear of explosion. They can be honest without triggering defensive reaction. His steadiness creates an environment where others can be themselves.

He becomes trustworthy. People follow leaders they trust, and trust requires consistency. The leader who reacts differently depending on his mood is impossible to trust fully, you never know which version of him you're dealing with. But the

leader who responds consistently, whose emotions are felt but don't drive erratic behavior, becomes someone people can rely on.

He becomes clear under pressure. When chaos rises, the emotionally mature man doesn't add to the chaos, he provides stability within it. He can think when others are panicking. He can respond when others are reacting. He can lead when others are frozen. Pressure reveals the value of the work he's done in quieter times.

He becomes difficult to manipulate. The man controlled by his emotions can be manipulated by anyone who knows how to trigger them. Make him angry enough and he'll say things he regrets. Make him afraid enough and he'll comply with things he shouldn't. Make him insecure enough and he'll compromise to gain approval. But the man whose emotions are felt but not followed is remarkably hard to manipulate. His responses come from conviction, not reaction.

Proverbs again:

"Better a patient person than a warrior, one with self-control than one who takes a city."
Proverbs 16:32

"Better than a warrior. Better than one who captures a city." This is how highly Scripture regards self-control: as a greater strength than military victory. The man who rules his own spirit has accomplished something more difficult and more valuable than conquest over external enemies. That man is ready for whatever the arena brings.

* * *

The work I did after that conversation with my mother, the honest examination of my patterns, the development of awareness, the practice of pause, the breaking of old agreements, didn't make me emotionless. I still feel frustration. I still feel anger. I still experience the full range of emotions that come with being human and engaged in life.

But something fundamental shifted. The emotions no longer drive the car. They're passengers, important passengers with valuable information to share, but passengers nonetheless. I decide where we're going. I decide how we respond to what's happening on the road. The emotions contribute to the conversation; they don't control the direction.

My family noticed the change before I did. "You're steadier," they said one day after a situation that would have triggered me in the past but didn't this time. "I can tell you still felt something, but you stayed with us instead of reacting." That's what emotional control looks like from the outside: steadiness that doesn't mean numbness, feeling that doesn't mean reactivity, strength that creates safety rather than volatility.

So here's the question I want you to sit with:

What emotional pattern most consistently undermines your leadership, your relationships, or your walk with God, and what would change if you mastered it instead of being mastered by it?

You probably know the pattern. Maybe it's anger that flares disproportionately. Maybe it's fear that drives avoidance. Maybe it's insecurity that creates defensiveness. Maybe it's frustration that produces withdrawal. Whatever it is, it's costing you something, in your relationships, in your leadership, in your integrity, in your peace.

Name it. Understand what triggers it. Develop the practices that build your capacity to respond rather than react. And become the steady man that the arena needs and that the people in your life deserve.

Strong men feel deeply. Strong men don't get ruled by what they feel. Join their ranks.

CHAPTER SIXTEEN

The Grind of Consistency

"Let us not become weary in doing good, for at the proper time we will reap a harvest if we do not give up."

Galatians 6:9

* * *

The turn came without fanfare.

I had been practicing a particular discipline for months, showing up every day, doing the work, seeing no visible progress. Each individual session felt insignificant. The effort seemed disconnected from any result. More than once I questioned whether the consistency was producing anything or just consuming time that could be spent on something more immediately rewarding. The grind felt pointless.

Then one day, without any single dramatic moment triggering it, I realized something had shifted. The capacity I had been developing was there. The change I had been working toward had happened, not suddenly but incrementally, invisibly, through the accumulated effect of showing up again and again. Looking back, I couldn't point to the day the transformation occurred because it hadn't occurred on any particular day. It had occurred across all the days, in the compound interest of consistent effort.

That season tested me more than any dramatic crisis could have. Crisis at least has adrenaline, urgency, a clear enemy to fight. But the grind has none of that. The grind is just showing up again to do the same things you did yesterday, trusting that the accumulation will eventually produce something even though you can't see it yet. The grind is waking up and choosing obedience when every feeling says it isn't working. The grind is faithfulness without feedback.

What I learned in that season changed how I understand growth: consistency is the multiplier that makes everything else work, but consistency doesn't feel powerful while you're living it. It feels like a grind. And the grind is where God does His deepest work, precisely because the grind is where everything except genuine faith and obedience gets stripped away.

Why Intensity Isn't Enough

Many men operate in bursts. They get inspired, make dramatic commitments, work with intense energy for a period, and then burn out, lose momentum, and drift until the next burst of inspiration arrives. The pattern repeats: intensity, exhaustion, drift, intensity, exhaustion, drift. They mistake the heat of the moment for meaningful progress.

Intensity feels powerful. It burns hot and gets attention. In the moment of intense effort, you feel like you're making significant progress. But intensity without consistency is like starting a fire without maintaining it, the initial blaze is impressive, but it produces no lasting warmth. Consistency is what maintains the fire over time, what produces the sustained heat that actually transforms things.

Paul used athletic imagery to describe his approach:

"Do you not know that in a race all the runners run, but only one gets the prize? Run in such a way as to get the prize. Everyone who competes in the games goes into strict training. They do it to get a crown that will not last, but we do it to get a crown that will last forever."
1 Corinthians 9:24-25

Strict training. Not occasional bursts of effort but sustained discipline over time. The crown goes not to the one who starts fastest but to the one who trains consistently and finishes faithfully. The man who shows up daily with moderate talent will eventually surpass the man who shows up occasionally with exceptional talent. Daily effort compounds in ways sporadic brilliance cannot.

How Small Things Compound

People chase huge wins, the turn moment, the dramatic transformation, the single decision that changes everything. But huge wins are built on small habits repeated relentlessly. Greatness is the product of repeated small moments executed faithfully.

Consider what happens when you read Scripture for fifteen minutes each day. Any single session seems insignificant, what difference can fifteen minutes make? But over a month, that's seven and a half hours with God's Word. Over a year, ninety hours. Over a decade, nine hundred hours of Scripture saturating your mind. The daily fifteen minutes didn't feel transformative, but the accumulation is profound.

The same is true for any discipline: a daily prayer, a daily workout, a daily moment of honest reflection. Each individual instance seems small. But small actions compound. They build on each other. They create momentum that carries you further than any single effort could. And crucially, they create neural pathways, spiritual habits, ingrained patterns that become automatic over time. The discipline that was hard at first becomes natural through repetition.

Jesus taught this principle when discussing faithfulness:

> *"Whoever can be trusted with very little can also be trusted with much, and whoever is dishonest with very little will also be dishonest with much."* ***Luke 16:10***

Very little. The small things. The seemingly insignificant daily choices. These are where trustworthiness is built or destroyed. The man who is faithful with small things, the daily prayer, the daily discipline, the daily choice to show up, demonstrates the character that qualifies him for larger things. Faithfulness in very little is the training ground for faithfulness in much.

This connects to everything we discussed in Chapter Seven about habits. The habits you build are consistent small actions that compound over time. This chapter extends that principle: the habits themselves must be maintained with relentless consistency for the compounding to work. Sporadic habits don't compound; they restart from zero each time. Only consistent habits build on themselves.

What the Grind Actually Feels Like

Here's what no one tells you about consistency: it rarely feels meaningful while you're living it. Consistency is the strategy; the grind is the experience. And the experience is harder than the strategy sounds.

The grind includes pain. You don't grow without discomfort, not real growth. Growth requires stretching beyond your current capacity, confronting things about yourself you'd rather avoid, sacrificing comfort for development. The pain doesn't mean something is wrong; it means something is forming.

The grind includes slowness. Growth is slow before it's fast. We love the fast part, the turn, the sudden progress, the moment when what was hard becomes natural. We hate the slow part, the months of invisible accumulation, the daily effort that seems to produce nothing. But the slow part is where the actual building happens. The fast part is just when it becomes visible.

The grind includes monotony. There's nothing exciting about doing the same disciplines day after day. The novelty wears off quickly. What remains is repetition, the same prayers, the same practices, the same confrontations with the same weaknesses. This monotony is not a bug in the growth process; it's the process itself. Repetition is how patterns get established, how character gets formed, how transformation moves from intention to identity.

James understood this:

"Consider it pure joy, my brothers and sisters, whenever you face trials of many kinds, because you know that the testing of your faith produces perseverance. Let perseverance finish its work so that you may be mature and complete, not lacking anything." James 1:2-4

"Let perseverance finish its work." The grind is perseverance doing its work, and that work takes time. James doesn't promise instant maturity. He says perseverance must be allowed to finish its work. Cutting the grind short means remaining incomplete.

What the Grind Exposes

The grind has a way of revealing you. When you're tired, frustrated, overwhelmed, discouraged, and not seeing results, that's when your true character appears. The grind doesn't create your character; it exposes it. And what gets exposed can then be addressed.

The grind exposes your commitment level. Are you interested or committed?

Chapter Nine drew that distinction, but the grind is where the answer becomes clear. Interest evaporates when the grind gets hard. Commitment persists because commitment doesn't depend on how you feel.

The grind exposes your blind spots. Weaknesses that stay hidden when life is easy surface when life is hard. Emotional immaturity, spiritual shallowness, mental drift, lazy habits, buried insecurity, the grind forces these to the surface. This exposure isn't punishment; it's a gift. You can't address what you can't see.

The grind exposes your dependence patterns. When the grind gets hard, what do you turn to? Some men turn to escapes, substances, entertainment, distractions that numb the discomfort. Some men turn to complaining, rehearsing grievances rather than pressing forward. Some men turn to God, discovering that the grind is producing a deeper dependence than they knew they needed. What you turn to under pressure reveals what you actually trust.

What Sustains You Through the Grind

Understanding that the grind is normal doesn't automatically make it endurable. You need resources, specific things that sustain you when the process is painful and the results are invisible.

Vision sustains you. Remembering what you're growing toward, the man you're becoming, the calling you're preparing for, the impact that's being shaped through the process, helps you endure the present difficulty. The grind feels meaningless when disconnected from purpose. Connect it to your larger vision, and the same grind becomes meaningful suffering rather than pointless pain.

Community sustains you. You need brothers who will journey with you, encourage you when you want to quit, correct you when you drift, remind you of the vision when you've forgotten it. The grind becomes unbearable alone; it becomes manageable with brothers who remind you of truth when your feelings tell lies.

Scripture sustains you. The truth of God's Word provides stability when your circumstances provide none. The stories of others who endured, Moses in the wilderness, David in the caves, Joseph in prison, remind you that the grind is part of God's pattern, not evidence of His absence. The man who lets Scripture go during the grind loses his anchor precisely when he needs it most.

Rest sustains you. The grind is not sustainable without recovery. Your body needs sleep. Your mind needs Sabbath. Your spirit needs restoration. The man who grinds without rest doesn't demonstrate superior commitment, he demonstrates poor stewardship. Build rest into the rhythm, and the grind becomes sustainable over the long term.

Identity sustains you. "I'm a man who shows up" is a reason to show up regardless of what you see happening. Your identity, who you are in Christ, what you've committed to, who you're becoming, provides motivation that doesn't depend on visible results. When results are invisible, identity keeps you moving.

Grace in the Grind

Here's a tension that must be held carefully: the grind requires effort, but it's not pure self-effort. Grace and grind coexist; in fact, they depend on each other.

Grace means you're not grinding to earn God's acceptance. You already have it through Christ. The grind isn't payment for salvation; it's response to salvation.

You're not working to make God love you; you're working because God already loves you and is forming you into someone who reflects that love.

Grace means the grind isn't in your power alone. Paul described this partnership:

"To this end I strenuously contend with all the energy Christ so powerfully works in me." Colossians 1:29

Paul strenuously contended, that's grind language, effort language, work language. But the energy wasn't his own; it was Christ powerfully working in him. You bring the effort; Christ provides the power. You show up and do the work; the transformation is beyond what your effort could produce alone.

Grace means failure in the grind isn't final. You will have days when you don't show up, when discipline breaks, when you fall short of what you intended. Grace

says those failures don't define you and don't disqualify you. You confess, receive forgiveness, and get back to the grind. The grace-filled grind says failure is part of the process and doesn't have the last word.

Holding grace and grind together protects you from two errors. All grind without grace produces burnout, anxiety, and performance-based spirituality. All grace without grind produces passivity, excuses, and shallow faith. The man in the arena needs both.

God's Pattern of Grinding Development

Look at how God shaped the men He used most significantly. Without exception, they went through extended grind seasons, unglamorous years of hidden development, before their visible impact began.

Moses spent forty years in the wilderness before the burning bush. Forty years of tending sheep in obscurity after being raised in Pharaoh's palace. What did those years produce? The death of his self-sufficiency. The development of patience he would desperately need when leading a complaining people through another wilderness. The grind prepared what the palace never could.

David was anointed king as a teenager, then spent years running from Saul, hiding in caves, leading a ragged band of misfits. Those years weren't a detour from his calling; they were preparation for it. In the caves, David learned to depend on God when every circumstance screamed that God had forgotten him. The Psalms that have sustained millions were written in those grind years, not in the comfort of the palace.

Joseph endured thirteen years between his dreams and their fulfillment, years of slavery and imprisonment, of faithfulness without reward. What did those years produce? The character that could handle the power he would eventually receive. Joseph told his brothers, "You intended to harm me, but God intended it for good." He could only say that because the grind had formed him.

If you're in an extended period of invisible development, you're in good company. If the growth feels slow and the impact feels nonexistent, you're walking the same path as men God used to change history. The grind isn't a sign that God has forgotten you, it's evidence that He's preparing you for something that requires this level of formation.

When the Pattern Collapses

Perhaps you've experienced seasons of consistency followed by seasons of complete collapse. You had the rhythm, you were showing up, you were seeing the compound effect begin, and then something happened and it all fell apart. Understanding why consistency breaks down helps you rebuild it.

Sometimes consistency breaks because of circumstances beyond your control. Illness, crisis, major life transitions can disrupt even the most established patterns. In these seasons, grace is required. Not every season of life allows for the same level of consistency. The goal is to maintain what you can and rebuild the rest when the season allows.

Sometimes consistency breaks because of drift. You missed one day, which made it easier to miss the next, which made it easier to miss the next, until the pattern had dissolved without any conscious decision to abandon it. Drift is insidious because it happens so gradually that you don't notice until you're far from where you started. The antidote to drift is awareness and quick correction when you notice you're slipping.

Sometimes consistency breaks because of isolation. When no one knows whether you're showing up, the temptation to skip increases. The accountability we discussed earlier serves consistency: when someone will ask how your disciplines are going, you're more likely to maintain them.

Sometimes consistency breaks because the pattern was too ambitious. You committed to more than you could sustain, and the unsustainable pace eventually collapsed. Better to commit to a modest pattern you can actually maintain than an impressive pattern you'll abandon within weeks. Sustainable consistency trumps impressive inconsistency.

Whatever caused the breakdown, the path forward is the same: start again. Not with guilt about the past, not with grand promises about the future, but with simple action today. Show up now. Then show up tomorrow. The streak restarts when you restart. Consistency doesn't require a perfect record, it requires discipline, not perfection. The goal isn't a flawless streak; it's a sustained direction.

Why Consistency Is Dangerous

The enemy doesn't fear the emotional Christian who burns hot for a season and then goes cold. He doesn't fear the impulsive man who makes dramatic commitments he won't keep. He doesn't fear the inconsistent leader whose impact is erased by his unreliability. He fears the man who keeps showing up.

The consistent man is dangerous because he can't be waited out. The enemy's strategy with many men is simply patience, wait for the enthusiasm to fade, wait for the effort to slacken, wait for the drift to do its work. But the consistent man doesn't fade. He keeps praying. He keeps obeying. He keeps building. He keeps fighting. He's still there next week, next month, next year. Patience doesn't defeat him because his showing up isn't dependent on temporary enthusiasm.

The consistent man is dangerous because he compounds. Each day of faithfulness builds on the last. His prayer life deepens over time. His knowledge of Scripture grows. His character develops. His influence expands. The enemy understands compound interest, small consistent deposits creating substantial accounts over time. A man who is consistently faithful for decades becomes a formidable force.

The consistent man is dangerous because he's unshakeable. He's not dependent on circumstances being favorable, on feelings cooperating, on motivation being present. He shows up regardless. He acts from commitment, not emotion. This kind of man is hard to manipulate, hard to discourage, hard to derail. He's grounded, focused, steady, aligned, and that makes him a threat to everything that depends on men being unstable.

The writer of Hebrews described this posture:

"Therefore, since we are surrounded by such a great cloud of witnesses, let us throw of everything that hinders and the sin that so easily entangles. And let us run with perseverance the race marked out for us, fixing our eyes on Jesus, the pioneer and perfecter of faith." Hebrews 12:1-2

"Run with perseverance." Not run with occasional bursts. Not run when you feel like it. Persevere, sustained effort over time, eyes fixed on Jesus, steady progress toward the goal. This is what relentless consistency looks like: a race run not in dramatic sprints but in faithful endurance.

* * *

That turn I described at the beginning, months of invisible effort, disciplines maintained without visible fruit, eventually produced what I couldn't see while I was in it. The turn, when it came, felt sudden, but it wasn't sudden at all. It was the accumulated result of every day I showed up when nothing seemed to be happening.

Looking back, I'm grateful for the grind, not because it was pleasant, but because it formed things in me that pleasant seasons never could. The depth, the discipline, the grit, the dependence on God, all of it was forged in unglamorous days of faithful obedience without reward. The grind was holy ground, even when it felt like wasteland.

The arena belongs to men who embrace the grind of consistency. Not men who merely endure it, resenting every day until it's over, but men who embrace it, who understand that this is where God shapes warriors, where character is forged, where the man you're becoming is actually built. The man who embraces the grind becomes unstoppable, consistent, dangerous. He becomes the man God designed him to be.

So here's the question I want you to sit with:

What grind are you currently in, and what would change if you stopped resenting it and started trusting that every day of faithfulness is producing something in you, even when you can't see it yet?

The grind is not pointless. It's the process that produces the man you're meant to become.

CHAPTER SEVENTEEN

Leading Yourself First

"He must manage his own family well and see that his children obey him, and he must do so in a manner worthy of full respect. (If anyone does not know how to manage his own family, how can he take care of God's church?)"

1 Timothy 3:4-5

* * *

I was leading others before I had learned to lead myself.

On the surface, things looked right. I had responsibility, influence, people who looked to me for direction. I gave advice about discipline while my own disciplines were eroding. I taught about emotional control while my own emotions were often running unchecked at home. I called others to consistency while my private life was marked by inconsistency I hoped no one would notice. The gap between my public leadership and my private reality was growing, and I kept hoping I could close it before anyone discovered the truth.

The discovery came not through dramatic exposure but through slow erosion of effectiveness. The people I was leading began to sense something was off. Not because they knew the specifics but because leadership cannot be compartmentalized forever. The disorder in my private life leaked into my public leading. My inconsistency created an instability that others could feel even if they couldn't name it. My credibility, built on what people saw publicly, was being undermined by who I was privately.

The turning point came when I finally admitted the obvious: I couldn't lead others to places I wasn't going myself. I couldn't call people to discipline I wasn't practicing. I couldn't inspire emotional steadiness I hadn't developed. I couldn't build on a foundation I hadn't laid in my own life. Leadership doesn't start withpeople, it starts with you. If you can't lead yourself, you can't lead anyone else. Not effectively. Not sustainably. Not with integrity.

What followed was a season of rebuilding from the inside out. Instead of trying to lead others while neglecting myself, I focused on leading myself first. The habits, the disciplines, the emotional work, the accountability, all of it applied to me before I tried to apply it to anyone else. And something remarkable happened: as my self-leadership strengthened, my leadership of others became more effective without me trying harder at it. The foundation I was building internally was expressing itself externally. Self-leadership was the lever that lifted everything else.

You Are Your First Assignment

Before God trusts you with people, He trusts you with you. Your first mission isn't leading a team, building an organization, or influencing a movement. Your first mission is stewarding the man God gave you to manage, your discipline, your habits, your mindset, your emotional life, your spiritual depth, your integrity. This is your primary assignment, and it remains your primary assignment even after other assignments are added.

Paul understood this when he described his own approach to ministry:

"No, I strike a blow to my body and make it my slave so that after I have preached to others, I myself will not be disqualified for the prize." 1 Corinthians 9:27

Paul preached to others, but his concern was that he himself would not be disqualified. His leadership of others didn't exempt him from leading himself. In fact, his leadership of others made self-leadership more critical, not less. The man who preaches to others while failing to discipline himself faces a unique danger: disqualification not from lack of talent but from lack of self-management.

This is why Scripture sets the bar for leadership at household management:

"He must manage his own family well and see that his children obey him, and he must do so in a manner worthy of full respect. If anyone does not know how to manage his own family, how can he take care of God's church?" 1 Timothy 3:4-5

The logic is plain: if you cannot manage your own household, the smallest circle of your responsibility, how can you be trusted with larger circles? And behind household management is self-management. The man who cannot lead himself cannot lead his family; the man who cannot lead his family cannot lead the church. Each circle depends on the circles within it, and self-leadership is the innermost circle on which all others depend.

The Integration of Everything

Throughout this book, we've explored many disciplines: identity, confession, battling fear, intentional living, habits, accountability, commitment, emotional control, temptation, responsibility, consistency. Each is valuable. But self-leadership is what integrates them into a unified whole.

You can practice individual disciplines in isolation, picking them up and putting them down depending on mood or circumstance. But self-leadership means treating your entire life as something you're responsible for leading. It means all the disciplines work together, reinforcing each other, creating a coherent way of living rather than a collection of disconnected practices.

Consider how the themes connect. Your identity, Chapter Two, determines who you're leading yourself to become. Confession, Chapter Four, keeps you honest about where you're actually falling short. Habits, Chapter Seven, are the daily practices through which you lead yourself. Accountability, Chapter Eight, provides external support for your internal leadership. Emotional control, Chapter Fifteen, is leading your reactions rather than being led by them. And, consistency is maintaining your self-leadership over time.

Self-leadership is not another discipline to add to the list. It's the posture that holds all the disciplines together. It's treating yourself as someone you're responsible to lead, with intention, strategy, accountability, and grace, rather than someone who just happens to do certain practices sometimes.

The man who leads himself asks different questions than the man who merely practices occasional disciplines. He asks: Where am I taking myself? What kind of

man am I forming through my choices? Where are the gaps between who I'm called to be and who I'm actually becoming? What needs to change, and what's my plan for changing it? These are leadership questions, and they're directed at yourself before they're directed at anyone else.

What Leading Yourself Requires

Self-leadership cannot be outsourced. You can delegate tasks and share responsibilities, but no one can lead your life for you. No one can pray for you, read Scripture for you, grow for you, change your habits for you, or obey for you. These are personal. The weight of self-leadership is one you must carry yourself.

Self-leadership requires brutal honesty. You cannot lead yourself if you keep lying to yourself about where you actually are. As we discussed in confession, Chapter Four, you must be honest about your weaknesses, your temptations, your inconsistencies, your avoidance patterns, your emotional triggers. Denial keeps you stuck; only truth gives you direction. The man who leads himself sees himself clearly, not with self-condemnation but with the honest assessment that accurate navigation requires.

Self-leadership requires standards. If you lead yourself according to emotion, doing what you feel like when you feel like it, you will drift with your moods. But if you lead yourself according to standards, clear commitments about who you will be and what you will do regardless of feeling, you have something to lead toward. Your standards should reflect your calling, your values, your spiritual identity, your long-term vision. They become the target you're leading yourself toward even when motivation is absent.

Self-leadership requires self-confrontation. Sometimes the biggest obstacle in your life is you, your excuses, your laziness, your fears, your comfort-seeking.

Leading yourself means confronting the man who hides behind those patterns. It means being willing to challenge yourself as honestly as you would challenge someone you were leading. You cannot grow a man you refuse to confront.

Self-leadership requires spiritual anchoring. Here's the critical distinction:

self-leadership is not self-help. Self-help says you have everything you need withinyourself; just dig deeper and try harder. But self-leadership rooted in self-effort alone burns out. Sustainable self-leadership is anchored in God's strength, directed by God's Spirit, aligned with God's purposes. It's not independence from God but deeper dependence on Him. The man who leads himself well knows he cannot do it in his own power, and that admission is what opens him to the power that actually sustains.

A Lifelong Practice

Self-leadership is not a phase you complete before moving on to leading others. It's a continuous practice that runs parallel to whatever else you're leading for the rest of your life. You never graduate from self-leadership. You never reach a point where you can stop leading yourself and focus only on leading others.

In fact, the more you lead others, the more critical your self-leadership becomes. Leadership brings unique pressures and temptations that require increased self-management, not less. The leader who thinks he has arrived, who stops actively leading himself because he's focused on leading others, is positioning himself for failure.

Consider David. He was a man after God's own heart, anointed king, successful in battle, leading a nation. And in a season when kings went off to war, David stayed home. His self-leadership slipped, he was idle when he should havebeen engaged, alone when he should have been with his men, and from that platform of compromised self-leadership came the disaster with Bathsheba. A man who had led armies and killed giants fell because he stopped leading himself in an unguarded moment.

The consequences didn't stay private. David's failure of self-leadership created consequences that rippled through his family and his nation for generations. His son Amnon. His son Absalom. The dysfunction that followed traced back to a king who, in a critical moment, stopped leading himself.

This is why self-leadership can never be completed. Every season brings new challenges. Every stage of life brings new temptations. Every level of influence brings new pressures. The man who led himself well at thirty must continue leading himself at forty, fifty, sixty, adjusting his self-leadership to address whatever that season requires. It's not a box to check; it's a continuous practice that ends only when life ends.

The Dangers Leadership Brings

Leadership itself creates specific temptations that require vigilant self-leadership to navigate. The man who leads others faces dangers that the man who leads only himself does not.

Pride is the first danger. When people follow you, listen to you, respect you, it's easy to start believing you deserve it, that there's something special about you that sets you apart. Pride blinds you to your weaknesses, makes you resistant to correction, and convinces you that the rules that apply to others don't apply to you. Self-leadership for the leader includes actively combating pride, staying in communities where you're challenged rather than just affirmed, remembering that any capacity you have is a gift, not an achievement.

Isolation is the second danger. Leaders often find themselves alone, at the top of organizations, carrying burdens they can't share with those they lead, unable to be vulnerable about struggles without undermining confidence. This isolation makes self-leadership harder because you lose the external input that helps you see yourself clearly. Self-leadership for the leader includes intentionally maintaining relationships where you're not in charge, where you can be peer or learner rather than always leader.

Entitlement is the third danger. The more you give, the more you can feel you're owed. The more you sacrifice for others, the more you can justify small compromises as compensation you deserve. Self-leadership for the leader includes recognizing entitlement when it arises and refusing to let sacrifice become justification for compromise.

Neglect of the basics is the fourth danger. When you're focused on leading others, the fundamental disciplines of your own life can slip. Prayer becomes rushed or absent. Scripture reading becomes preparation for teaching rather than food for your own soul. Rest becomes optional. Exercise stops. The basics you would counselothers to maintain become the things you neglect while serving them. Self-leadership for the leader includes protecting the foundations of your own life with the same intensity you bring to your leadership.

What Leading Yourself Produces

The man who leads himself well develops qualities that make his leadership of others more effective, not through techniques or strategies but through the overflow of who he's become.

Self-leadership produces stability. A man who leads himself is steady. He thinks clearly because his mind is ordered. He responds calmly because his emotions are managed. He acts consistently because his habits are established. This stability becomes something others can depend on. People follow leaders they can rely on, and reliability is built through self-leadership.

Self-leadership produces authority. Not the authority of position or title, but the authority of integrity. People naturally trust and follow men who manage themselves, honor their word, walk in truth, and master their impulses. This authority is earned privately, in the self-leadership no one sees, and recognized publicly. You cannot manufacture it through charisma; you can only build it through character.

Self-leadership produces overflow. When you lead yourself well, you have something to give. Your peace overflows into how you lead others. Your wisdom, accumulated through disciplined self-development, overflows into the counsel you offer. Your clarity, maintained through guarding your mind, overflows into the direction you provide. You lead from abundance rather than emptiness. The man who neglects his own soul while leading others eventually runs dry; the man who tends his soul has renewable resources to share.

Self-leadership produces credibility. You can lead people to places you've actually been. When you call others to discipline, you speak from experience of discipline. When you call others to perseverance, you speak from having persevered. When you call others to obedience, you speak from walking in obedience yourself.

This credibility cannot be faked; people eventually sense the difference between a leader who lives what he teaches and one who merely talks about it.

When Self-Leadership Has Failed

Perhaps you're reading this chapter aware that your self-leadership has failed, perhaps publicly, perhaps with consequences for your leadership of others. The gap between who you were supposed to be and who you actually were has been exposed. The credibility you once had has been damaged. What now?

The path forward begins with genuine repentance, not just regret that you were caught or that there are consequences, but actual turning. This connects to everything we discussed in Chapter Four about confession. Own what happened. Don't minimize, don't deflect, don't manage the narrative. Let the failure be seen for what it was.

After repentance comes rebuilding, which starts with self-leadership before it extends back to leadership of others. You may need a season where you're not leading others at all, where your only focus is re-establishing the foundation that collapsed. This feels like demotion, but it's actually proper order. You cannot rebuild your leadership of others until you've rebuilt your leadership of yourself.

The credibility that was lost will not return quickly. Others are right to watch and wait, to see whether change is real before extending trust again. Accept this as appropriate rather than resenting it. Credibility is rebuilt through sustained demonstration, not through declarations of change. Time and consistency are required; there are no shortcuts.

Peter denied Jesus three times, a catastrophic failure of self-leadership in the moment it mattered most. But Peter's story didn't end with failure. He was restored,

recommissioned, and became a pillar of the church. His earlier failure didn't disqualify his later faithfulness. If you've failed in self-leadership, you're not disqualified. But you must do the work of rebuilding, starting with leading yourself before leading anyone else.

* * *

The season I described at the beginning of this chapter, when I was leading others while failing to lead myself, was painful to confront. But confronting it was the beginning of becoming the leader I was supposed to be. The rebuilding was slow. The changes were internal before they were visible. But eventually, the self-leadership that had been missing became the foundation for leadership that was more effective, more sustainable, more full of integrity than anything I had offered before.

Every man wants influence. Every man wants impact. Every man wants to lead in some sphere, a family, a team, an organization, a community. But leadership doesn't start with people. It starts with you. The man who leads himself well has something to offer. The man who neglects his own leadership while focusing on others eventually has nothing to give.

The arena belongs to men who lead themselves first. Not perfectly, we've established that perfection isn't the standard, but intentionally, consistently, honestly. Men who treat themselves as the first assignment God has given them. Men who understand that self-leadership is not selfish but foundational. Men who know that everything they build, everything they influence, everything they touch is shaped by the leadership they practice privately before anyone is watching.

So here's the question I want you to sit with:

Where is your self-leadership strongest, where is it weakest, and what would change in your leadership of others if you addressed the weakness?

You already know. There's an area where you're leading yourself well and it's producing fruit. There's another area where your self-leadership is compromised and it's leaking into everything else. Name both. Celebrate the strength, but don't let it

distract you from the weakness. The weakness is where the work needs to happen, where the next level of your leadership, of others and of yourself, will be unlocked.

Lead yourself first. Lead yourself with clarity, courage, discipline, and integrity. And from that foundation, lead everything else you've been entrusted to lead.

That's the blueprint. That's the path. That's how men who change

the world actually do it.

CHAPTER EIGHTEEN

The Arena Mindset

"It is not the critic who counts; not the man who points out how the strong man stumbles, or where the doer of deeds could have done them better. The credit belongs to the man who is actually in the arena."

Theodore Roosevelt

* * *

We began this book with an invitation and a question.

The invitation was to step into the arena, to leave the stands where critics sit safely, where life is observed rather than lived, where comfort is preserved at the cost of impact. The question was whether you would accept that invitation or continue watching from the sidelines while other men fought the battles that matter.

Now, having journeyed through these chapters together, you've been equipped for that arena. You've examined your identity and learned that who you are must come before what you do. You've confronted the fight within and discovered that the greatest battles are internal. You've learned the power of confession and the freedom it brings. You've faced fear, doubt, and comparison and found they can be defeated.

You've built frameworks for intentional living, daily habits, and accountability. You've distinguished interest from commitment and discovered where greatness lives.

You've developed the discipline of focus and learned the power of standing firm. You've learned to guard your mind, face temptation, and control your emotions. You've shouldered responsibility and discovered it forms rather than crushes. You've embraced the grind of consistency and committed to the long game that builds lasting legacy. You've learned to lead yourself before leading others.

You're not the same man who started reading this book. You've been equipped. The question is no longer whether you have what it takes, it's whether you'll step in, stay in, and finish what you've begun.

The Mindset That Wins

The arena is unforgiving. It doesn't care about your intentions or your potential. It doesn't adjust its difficulty based on your feelings. It doesn't grade on a curve because you tried hard. The arena rewards one thing: the mindset you bring into it.

The arena mindset is the internal framework that keeps you grounded, focused, disciplined, and unshakeable when life applies pressure. It's not hype, hype fades when difficulty arrives. It's not emotion, emotion fluctuates too much to build on. It's not even talent, talent without the right mindset produces wasted potential. The arena mindset is something deeper: a way of seeing, thinking, and responding that makes everything else effective.

This mindset is the synthesis of everything we've explored. Identity anchors it, the man who knows who he is in Christ cannot be shaken by what the arena throws at him. Discipline structures it, the man who has built habits doesn't have to rely on how he feels in the moment. Responsibility empowers it, the man who owns his life rather than blaming circumstances has leverage others don't. Long-term thinking stabilizes it, the man who plays for decades rather than days isn't derailed by temporary setbacks.

Paul described his own arena mindset:

"I press on toward the goal to win the prize for which God has called me heavenward in Christ Jesus." Philippians 3:14

“I press on.” Not "I feel inspired" or "circumstances are favorable" or "people are supporting me." “I press on”, regardless of what I feel, regardless of what's happening around me, regardless of whether anyone is watching or applauding. The arena mindset presses on when everything in the natural world says stop.

What the Mindset Contains

The arena mindset contains certain convictions that become automatic responses under pressure.

It contains identity certainty. The man in the arena knows who he is, not based on performance or approval but based on what God has declared. When the arena attacks his worth, questions his calling, or whispers that he doesn't belong, he has an answer that doesn't depend on the arena's verdict. His identity is settled before he steps in.

It contains ownership mentality. The arena mindset removes blame from its vocabulary. It doesn't say "it's their fault" or "life is unfair" or "circumstances are holding me back." It says "I own my decisions, my habits, my discipline, my direction." Excuses are comfortable but powerless; ownership is uncomfortable but potent.

It contains action orientation. The arena mindset doesn't ask "Do I feel like it?" It asks "What does obedience require right now?" and then moves. Emotional men wait for motivation; arena men move without it. Action builds momentum that emotion alone cannot sustain.

It contains expectation of resistance. Weak men are shocked by adversity, as if difficulty were an aberration rather than the normal condition of life in the arena.

But the arena mindset expects resistance. It says: "Pressure is normal. Challenges are training. Difficulty is expected." When you expect resistance, you stop being discouraged by it and start being strengthened through it.

It contains truth as the foundation. The arena mindset bases decisions on Scripture, conviction, integrity, and wisdom, not on emotional impulses that change by the hour. Truth anchors you when your feelings betray you.

It contains commitment to finish. Starting is emotional; finishing is spiritual. The arena mindset isn't just about entering the fight, it's about staying until the end, completing what was begun, crossing the finish line rather than abandoning the race halfway through. This commitment to finish is what separates the man who makes an impact from the man who merely made an appearance.

Finishing the Fight

Anyone can start strong. Few finish strong. The world is full of talented starters who never become faithful finishers. The arena doesn't crown starters; it crowns finishers.

Finishing requires everything we've discussed: the identity that anchors you, the habits that sustain you, the accountability that supports you, the emotional control that steadies you, the focus that protects you, the consistency that compounds, the long-game thinking that keeps you going when results are invisible. All of it converges in the capacity to finish what you started.

Finishing requires outlasting resistance. Resistance never leaves; it evolves. Every new level attracts new attacks, new pressure, new temptations. The man who finishes isn't the man who eliminates resistance, that's impossible. He's the man who refuses to be worn down by it, who outlasts what he cannot defeat.

Finishing requires winning the internal battle. You don't finish because your schedule clears or your opposition disappears. You finish when you win the internal fight, against fatigue, against doubt, against fear, against the voice that says quitting would be easier. The internal war is the real war. The men who finish are the men who master themselves.

Finishing requires faith that carries you where flesh fails. Your strength isn't enough. Your willpower isn't enough. Faith says: "God is with me. God strengthens me. God finishes what He starts." Faith keeps you moving when nothing else does.

"Being confident of this, that he who began a good work in you will carry it on to completion until the day of Christ Jesus."
Philippians 1:6

He who began a good work will carry it on to completion. The God who started the work in you is committed to finishing it. Your role is cooperation, notself-reliance. You bring your obedience; He provides the power that makes completion possible.

"It Is Finished"

Jesus knew what finishing meant. His entire earthly ministry moved toward a completion that would cost Him everything.

In the garden of Gethsemane, facing the cross, He prayed for another way. "Father, if you are willing, take this cup from me." The humanity of Jesus experienced what we experience when finishing becomes unbearable: the desire for a different path. But His prayer continued: "Yet not my will, but yours be done." He submitted His desire to the Father's purpose and moved toward the finish.

On the cross, in His final moments, Jesus spoke words that echo through history:

"It is finished." John 19:30

“It is finished.” The work the Father gave Him to do, completed. The mission He came to accomplish, fulfilled. The race marked out for Him, run to the end.

Jesus didn't almost finish. He didn't get close and then stop. He finished. And in finishing, He accomplished what starting could never have accomplished.

This is the model for every man in the arena. Your assignment matters, but only if you complete it. Your calling is significant, but only if you see it through. "It is finished" isn't just Jesus' testimony, it's the goal for every follower of His.

Fighting, Finishing, Keeping

Near the end of his life, facing execution, Paul wrote words that every man in the arena should aspire to say:

> *"I have fought the good fight, I have finished the race, I have kept the faith. Now there is in store for me the crown of righteousness, which the Lord, the righteous Judge, will award to me on that day, and not only to me, but also to all who have longed for his appearing." 2 Timothy 4:7-8*

Three claims: “I have fought. I have finished. I have kept the faith.”

Fighting means engaging, not watching from the sidelines, not avoiding the difficulty, not choosing the comfortable path. Paul fought. He entered the arena. He faced opposition, persecution, hardship, betrayal. He didn't drift through life; he engaged it with everything he had.

Finishing means completing what was started. Paul didn't just fight occasionally; he fought to the end. The race wasn't abandoned halfway through. The mission wasn't traded for something easier. He saw it through.

Keeping the faith means maintaining integrity throughout. It's possible to fight and finish but lose your soul in the process, to compromise along the way, to cut corners, to finish but not finish well. Paul kept the faith. His finishing was characterized by faithfulness, not just completion.

And then: the crown of righteousness. This is what awaits the man who finishes. Not applause from the watching world, Paul was in prison awaiting execution, not receiving standing ovations. The crown comes from the Lord, the righteous Judge. The reward for finishing faithfully is eternal, not temporal.

When You Close This Book

You're about to close this book and return to your life. The question is what happens next. Knowledge without application is just information; it transforms nothing. What will you do with what you've learned?

Start with identity. If you haven't settled who you are in Christ, not based on performance but based on His declaration, nothing else will hold. Go back to that foundation. Write down what God says about you. Let it become the anchor on which everything else is built.

Build one habit at a time. Don't try to implement everything simultaneously, that's a recipe for overwhelm and abandonment. Choose one discipline. Establish it. Let it become automatic. Then add another. The man who builds slowly builds durably.

Find your brothers. You cannot do this alone. The fight within cannot be won in isolation. If you don't have brothers who will walk with you, challenge you, and hold you accountable, finding them is your immediate priority. Everything else becomes harder without community.

Choose the long game. Decide now that you're playing for decades, not days.

Let that commitment reframe how you approach the daily disciplines. You're not trying to feel good this week; you're building a man who will still be standing in thirty years.

Commit to finish. Not just to start well, not just to fight for a while, but to finish. Make the decision now, before the difficulty arrives, that you will see this through to the end. That pre-commitment will carry you through the moments when quitting seems reasonable.

And step into the arena. Not someday, not when you feel ready, not after you've achieved some imaginary level of preparation. Now. The arena is where the formation happens. You don't get ready and then enter; you enter and the entering makes you ready.

The Man Who Emerges

The man who develops the arena mindset and commits to finishing becomes something different, something the arena respects and darkness fears.

He becomes unshakeable. Not unfeeling, he experiences the full range of emotion, but unshakeable. His identity is anchored too deeply to be moved by circumstances. His convictions are settled too firmly to be swayed by pressure. He can be hurt but not defeated. He can be opposed but not derailed.

He becomes trustworthy. People can depend on him because he's consistent.

Leaders can entrust him with responsibility because he owns it. God can give him greater assignment because he's proven faithful with what he's already received.

He becomes dangerous, not to people, but to the forces that keep people bound. A man who cannot be manipulated emotionally or intimidated mentally becomes a problem for darkness. His stability threatens chaos. His clarity threatens confusion. His faithfulness threatens the entropy that would otherwise prevail.

He becomes a finisher. Not someone who started well once, but someone who sees things through. His life will be marked not by impressive beginnings but by faithful completions. And when his race is over, he'll be able to say what Paul said: I have fought. I have finished. I have kept the faith.

> *"Therefore, my dear brothers and sisters, stand firm. Let nothing move you. Always give yourselves fully to the work of the Lord, because you know that your labor in the Lord is not in vain." 1 Corinthians 15:58*

Welcome to the Arena

Roosevelt's words have echoed through this entire book, and they belong here at the end:

> *"It is not the critic who counts; not the man who points out how the strong man stumbles, or where the doer of deeds could have done them better. The credit belongs to the man who is actually in the arena, whose face is marred by dust and sweat and blood; who strives valiantly; who errs, who comes short again and again, because there is no effort without error and shortcoming; but who does actually strive to do the deeds; who knows great enthusiasms, the great*

devotions; who spends himself in a worthy cause; who at the best knows in the end the triumph of high achievement, and who at the worst, if he fails, at least fails while daring greatly, so that his place shall never be with those cold and timid souls who neither know victory nor defeat."
Theodore Roosevelt

The man in the arena. Face marred by dust and sweat and blood. Striving valiantly. Erring, coming short, but actually striving. Spending himself in a worthy cause. Daring greatly.

This is who you're called to be. Not perfect, the man in the arena errs and comes short. But present. Engaged. Fighting. Finishing.

The critics will always be there, in the stands, safe, pointing out how you could have done it better. Let them criticize. Their opinions don't count. What counts is whether you're in the arena, whether you showed up, whether you stayed, whether you finished.

You've been equipped. These chapters have prepared you. The identity, the disciplines, the mindset, they're available to you now. The only question remaining is the one we started with: Will you step in? Will you stay? Will you finish?

* * *

The arena is waiting.

It will be hard. It will cost you. It will demand everything you have and then ask for more. You will fail sometimes, come short again and again, as Roosevelt said. You will doubt yourself, wonder if you're enough, feel the weight of the fight pressing down on you.

For you will be alive in a way that the man in the stands will never experience. You will be building something that matters. You will be becoming someone worthy of the calling God has placed on your life. And at the end, whenever that end comes, you will be able to say what Paul said:

> *I have fought the good fight. I have finished the race. I have kept the faith. 2 Timothy 4:7*

That's the goal. That's the prize. That's what all of this has been preparing youfor.

So go. Enter the arena. Fight the fight. Finish the race. Keep the faith. Welcome to the arena, brother.

Now become the man you were created to be.

CHAPTER NINETEEN

The Arena Manifesto

"But be doers of the word, and not hearers only, deceiving yourselves."

James 1:22

* * *

I want to take you back to a hospital room in the summer afternoon.

That is where this book began. A father dying I'd resented most of my life. Relationships fracturing under years of my neglect. A business hemorrhaging because I was too proud to ask for help. A man performing the role of someone who had it together while everything underneath was coming apart.

That night, I made one decision. I decided to stop being a spectator in my own life. I decided to step into the arena.

Every chapter of this book has been the working out of that single decision. Identity before strategy. The fight within. Confession and correction. Disciplined habits. Focused refusal. A guarded mind. Emotional control. Relentless consistency. Self-leadership. Each one a piece of what it actually takes to be in the arena rather than just talk about it.

Now we close where the book began, but with what you did not have on the first page: a code.

Every man lives by a code, either intentionally or accidentally.

Most men never choose theirs. They drift into whatever mindset, habits, and beliefs their environment hands them. They become products of pressure instead of producers of purpose. Their code is written by default: by culture, by comfort, by the path of least resistance. And they wonder why their lives feel aimless, why they lack the grounding that men of impact seem to possess.

But men in the arena choose their code. They live by conviction, not convenience. By purpose, not preference. By discipline, not emotion. By truth, not trend. They have decided in advance who they will be, and that decision carries them through the moments when everything in them wants to become someone else.

What follows is a manifesto, not a slogan to repeat but a standard to live by. These declarations distill everything we've explored in this book into commitments you can claim as your own. They're not aspirations for someday; they're stakes in the ground for today. Each one represents a choice: the way of the arena versus the way of the stands, the path of purpose versus the drift of passivity.

I encourage you to do more than read these declarations. Speak them aloud. Return to them regularly, daily, if possible. Let them become the code that shapes your decisions when you're too tired to think clearly, too pressured to evaluate carefully, too tempted to choose wisely on your own. A manifesto does its workthrough repetition, through declaration, through the slow process of truth becoming reflex.

This is who you are choosing to become. These are the commitments that will carry you through the arena.

* * *

I Choose the Arena Over the Stands

I refuse to watch life from a distance. I will not spectate while others fight for their calling, their families, their faith. I step into the arena, into responsibility, into difficulty, into the fight that matters. My face will be marred by dust and sweat and blood. I will know victory and defeat. But I will not be numbered among those cold and timid souls who know neither.

I'm not hiding. I'm showing up.

I Choose Identity Over Image

I'm done pretending. Done performing. Done chasing approval that cannot satisfy. My identity comes from God, from what He declares, not what culture demands or comparison whispers or insecurity fears. I know who I am in Christ, and that knowledge anchors me when everything else shifts.

I lead from truth, not ego.

I Choose Purpose Over Comfort

Comfort is convenient. Purpose is costly. I choose the cost. I choose the stretching, the refining, the difficulty that produces something in me that ease never could. Comfort cannot transform me. Purpose can. I will not organize my life around avoiding discomfort; I will organize it around fulfilling my calling.

I was not made for comfort. I was made for purpose.

I Choose Discipline Over Emotion

My emotions are real, but they are not in charge. I will not be led by what I feel in the moment. I build my life on discipline: clear habits, grounded decisions, focused direction, consistent action. Discipline leads; emotion follows. When my feelings say stop, my discipline says continue. When my feelings say quit, my discipline says finish.

My commitments outweigh my moods.

I Choose Responsibility Over Excuses

Excuses are easy. Responsibility is rare. I choose responsibility. I own my actions, my habits, my direction, my outcomes. I release blame. I reject victimhood. I refuse to give my power away to circumstances, to other people's failures, to the unfairness of life. What I own, I can change. What I blame, I cannot.

I carry my weight with honor.

I Choose Truth Over Feelings

Feelings change by the hour. Truth does not. Scripture is my standard. Wisdom is my guide. Integrity is my boundary. When my feelings conflict with truth, truth wins. I will not build my life on the shifting sand of emotion; I will build it on the solid rock of what God has declared.

Truth anchors me when my emotions fluctuate.

I Choose Intentionality Over Drift

Drift destroys potential silently. I refuse to drift. I will think clearly, choose deliberately, plan strategically, act consistently. My life will not be accidental, shaped by whatever influences happen to be strongest. I will be the one shaping my life, under God's direction, through intentional choices made daily.

Where I end up will be where I aimed.

I Choose Brotherhood Over Isolation

Lone wolves die alone. Strong men build together. I choose accountability, support, honesty, challenge, encouragement. I will not fight this fight by myself. I will surround myself with brothers who sharpen me, who speak truth when I need to hear it, who pull me back when I drift and push me forward when I stall.

Iron sharpens iron. I need my brothers.

I Choose Resilience Over Quitting

When pressure hits, I won't fold. When fear rises, I won't run. When discouragement comes, I won't retreat. I will stand. I will endure. I will finish what I started. I have decided in advance: quitting is not my story. Faithfulness is. I may bend under the weight, but I will not break.

I finish what I start.

I Choose Obedience Over Outcome

I don't control results. I control obedience. God handles the outcome; I handle the alignment. My job is faithfulness, not success as the world measures it. I will obey regardless of whether the results come quickly, slowly, or not at all in my lifetime. My success is found in faithfulness, not applause.

Obedience is my responsibility. Outcome is God's.

I Choose Legacy Over Convenience

My life is not just about me. I am building for children and grandchildren who aren't born yet. I am breaking patterns that have run

through my family for generations. I am establishing patterns that will bless generations to come. What I do today echoes forward into lives I'll never meet.

Legacy is my responsibility. Legacy is my assignment.

I Choose the Long Game Over Instant Results

I'm not here for quick wins. I'm here for lasting impact. I choose patience, endurance, consistency, longevity. I measure by decades, not days. I build for the finish line, not the first mile. The long game builds the man the short game never could, and I'm playing the long game.

I'm still going to be here in thirty years.

I Choose Faith Over Fear

Fear whispers lies. Faith speaks truth. Fear shrinks my vision. Faith expands it. Fear paralyzes. Faith mobilizes. I walk by faith, not by sight. I fight by faith when my strength fails. I build by faith when results are invisible. I endure by faith when everything says quit. Faith is my fuel, and my faith is in the God who has never failed.

I will not be governed by fear.

I Choose Stability Over Chaos

Chaos is the world's rhythm. Stability is mine. I refuse emotional whiplash, mental instability, spiritual drift. I will be a steady presence in an unsteady world, grounded, consistent, reliable. When everything around me shakes, I will stand firm on the foundation that cannot be moved.

I am anchored. I am unmoved.

I Choose to Live as a Man in the Arena

This is not a moment. This is a lifestyle. This is not enthusiasm that fades. This is commitment that endures. I choose strength. I choose purpose. I choose clarity. I choose obedience. I choose discipline. I choose truth. I choose resilience. I choose growth. I choose God's calling over my comfort. I choose the arena.

I will hold the line.

* * *

These fifteen declarations are now your code. Not because you've read them, but because you've chosen them.

A manifesto does its work through repetition. I encourage you to return to these declarations regularly, daily, if possible. Read them aloud. Let them become familiar enough that they surface automatically when decisions arise. When you're tired and tempted to quit, let "I finish what I start" speak louder than your fatigue. When you're pressured to compromise, let "I choose truth over feelings" anchor you. When you're isolated and drifting, let "I need my brothers" move you toward community.

Consider sharing this manifesto with the brothers who are walking with you. Declare it together. Hold each other accountable to it. Let these commitments become the shared code of men who are choosing the arena over the stands.

The journey we've taken through this book, from entering the arena to finishing the fight, has equipped you with everything you need. The identity, the disciplines, the mindset, the community, the long-term vision, the commitment to finish. This manifesto gathers it all into declarations you can carry with you into every day, every decision, every battle.

You are a man in the arena now. Live like it. Fight like it.

Finish like it.

The arena is waiting. Your code is set. Your brothers are with you.

And, God goes before you.

Now go.

Acknowledgments

Books do not get written alone. Neither do men get forged alone. Both of those truths are on display in these pages.

To my father, Jim Holt. You are the reason this book exists and the reason I understand what redemption actually costs. God did something in us that neither of us deserved. I will spend the rest of my life grateful for it.

To the men who have walked with me through the years when none of this was visible. You know who you are. You showed up when I was not easy to be around, told me the truth when I did not want to hear it, and stayed when it would have been easier to leave. That is brotherhood. That is iron. Thank you.

To every man who has sat across from me in a coaching conversation, a mastermind session, or a hard conversation in a hospital waiting room. You trusted me with the real version of your life. That trust is not something I take lightly. Your willingness to step into the arena made me a better guide and a better man.

To the scholars and teachers whose work shapes how I think: Chuck Missler, David Pawson, and Michael Heiser. You taught me that theological rigor and genuine faith are not in competition. That lesson is in every chapter of this book whether I cite you directly or not.

Twenty-one years ago, someone handed me a reason to stay sober one more day. I do not know if they will ever read this. If they do: it worked. All of it.

And to the reader who made it this far. You did not have to finish. The fact that you did tells me something about you. Stay in the arena.

Also by Ryan Nelson Holt

The Arena Ledger

A Daily Reckoning for Men in the Arena

In the Arena gives you the framework. The Arena Ledger is where you do the daily work of living it out.

Built around the 7F Framework and the four phases of the day, the Ledger is a thirteen-week structured reckoning for men who are serious about closing the gap between conviction and conduct. Inside you will find a 12-Week Battle Plan with a Drift Inventory and Build Plan, daily work pages for each of the thirteen weeks, a Recurring Patterns section for tracking what surfaces under pressure, a Year in Ledger review, and the Arena Manifesto with space to write your own code alongside the fifteen declarations.

The Ledger is not a journal. It is a record of a man becoming who he said he wanted to be.

Discussion Questions

These questions are designed for men reading In the Arena together, whether in a small group, a mastermind, a men's ministry, or a one-on-one accountability relationship. Each set follows the chapter's central argument. Take your time with them. The goal is not to finish the list. The goal is to tell the truth.

Chapter One: In the Arena

1. When was the last time you were truly in the arena, not watching or commenting but actually in it? What did it cost you?

2. Ryan describes most men as circling the arena without stepping in. Where are you circling right now?

3. What is the specific arena God is calling you into that you have been avoiding? What is the real reason you have not stepped in?

Chapter Two: Identity Before Strategy

1. Ryan argues that identity must precede strategy. Where in your life have you been building strategy on an unstable identity?

2. What does your actual behavior reveal about what you believe about yourself, not what you say you believe?

3. If the men closest to you described your identity in three words, what would they say? Are those the words you would choose for yourself?

Chapter Three: The Fight Within

1. What internal battle are you currently fighting that no one around you knows about?

2. Ryan writes that you can conquer a room and still lose to yourself. Where is that true for you right now?

3. What have you been blaming on external circumstances that might actually be an internal problem?

Chapter Four: The Power of Confession and Correction

1. What have you been carrying alone that needs to be spoken out loud to another person?

2. Ryan describes confession as a discipline for warriors, not a sign of weakness. What is your honest reaction to that framing?

3. Is there a correction you have been avoiding because you already know what it will require you to change?

Chapter Five: Battling Fear, Doubt, and Comparison

1. Which of the three enemies, fear, doubt, or comparison, has the most power over you right now? Be specific.

2. Ryan nearly missed a defining opportunity because he spent three hours negotiating with fear. What opportunity are you currently negotiating around instead of stepping into?

3. Whose race are you measuring yourself against that you should stop watching?

Chapter Six: The Practice of Intentional Living

1. If you honestly evaluated the last ninety days, would you say you have been living intentionally or reactively?

2. Where has drift shown up in your life that you have been calling something else?

3. What one decision, made today, would most change the direction of your next twelve months?

Chapter Seven: The Importance of Daily Habits

1. What do your current daily habits reveal about what you actually value, not what you say you value?

2. Ryan traces significant transformation back to one fifteen-minute daily habit. What is the one small habit that, if practiced consistently, would change the most for you?

3. Which habit have you started and abandoned most often? What does that pattern tell you?

Chapter Eight: Accountability as Ownership

1. Do you have anyone in your life who can show up unannounced and ask you the hard questions? If not, why not?

2. Ryan was avoiding his accountability partner because he had nothing good to report. Where are you currently hiding from accountability?

3. What is the difference between the accountability you currently have and the accountability you actually need?

Chapter Nine: Interest vs. Commitment

1. Ryan's mentor asked: what have you actually sacrificed for the change you say you want? Answer that question honestly.

2. Where in your life are you interested in change but not yet committed to it? What would commitment actually require?

3. What do you need to stop adding to your life and start actually sacrificing?

Chapter Ten: Greatness in the Moment

1. Think of a moment in the last month that seemed insignificant at the time. In hindsight, what was actually at stake?

2. Where are you waiting for a dramatic defining moment when the real opportunity is in the ordinary one in front of you?

3. What commitment have you been close to breaking that is worth protecting?

Chapter Eleven: The Discipline of Focus

1. What good things are you currently doing that are actually preventing you from doing the essential things?

2. Ryan distinguishes between balance and priority. What would your life look like if you organized it around priority instead of balance?

3. What is the one thing, if you focused on it exclusively for the next ninety days, that would produce the most meaningful result?

Chapter Twelve: The Discipline of Standing Firm

1. Describe a season when everything in you wanted to retreat. What did you do? What would you do differently now?

2. What pressure are you currently under that is testing your ability to stand firm? What is it exposing about your foundation?

3. Ryan argues that standing firm is built before pressure arrives. What are you building right now that will hold when the next season of pressure comes?

Chapter Thirteen: Guarding Your Mind

1. What thoughts do you allow to run unchallenged that are costing you the most?

2. Ryan describes his mind as enemy territory. What lie has taken up residence in your thought life that you have not yet evicted?

3. What is your current practice for taking thoughts captive? Is it working?

Chapter Fourteen: Facing Temptation

1. Ryan writes that temptation arrives disguised as relief. What does temptation currently look like in your life?

2. In what area are you most depleted right now, and how is that depletion making you more vulnerable?

3. What structural safeguard do you need to put in place that you have been avoiding because it feels excessive?

Chapter Fifteen: Emotional Control

1. Who bears the cost of your emotional reactivity most often? Have you ever told them you know that?

2. What emotion do you suppress instead of lead? What does that cost you?

3. What would it look like to feel your emotions fully without letting them make your decisions?

Chapter Sixteen: The Grind of Consistency

1. What grind are you currently in? Be specific about what it feels like from the inside.

2. Ryan distinguishes between enduring the grind and embracing it. Which are you doing right now?

3. What would you need to believe about what God is doing in the invisible seasons to change how you show up in this one?

Chapter Seventeen: Leading Yourself First

1. Where is the gap between your public leadership and your private reality largest right now?

2. Ryan argues you cannot lead others to places you are not going yourself. Where has that proven true in your experience?

3. What would change in how you lead others if you focused entirely on leading yourself well for the next thirty days?

Chapter Eighteen: The Arena Mindset

1. Looking back over all the chapters, which discipline is most underdeveloped in your life right now?

2. The arena mindset is described as a way of seeing, thinking, and responding. What would need to change in how you currently see your circumstances to carry this mindset into the week ahead?

3. You are a different man than you were when you started this book. What has actually changed, and what are you still carrying from the stands?

Chapter Nineteen: The Arena Manifesto

1. Read the fifteen declarations aloud. Which one is the hardest for you to say and mean right now? Why?

2. Which declaration are you currently living most consistently? What built that in you?

3. Write your own declaration. One sentence. The commitment that is most personal to your arena right now, the one that, if you kept it, would change the most.

About the Author

Ryan Nelson Holt is the founder of RNH Media, a faith-driven leadership platform for Christian entrepreneurs, executives, and operators. He is the host of FORGED, a podcast built on the conviction that faith proven through disciplined execution is not a slogan but a way of life.

Ryan brings twenty-one years of sobriety, a career in regulated financial services, and the hard-won clarity of a man who has built and led under genuine constraint to everything he writes and teaches. He is not writing from theory. He is writing from the forge.

He works with men through The Foundry, a membership community for Thinking Christian Operators, and the Redemption Mastermind, a twelve-week cohort for leaders who are serious about closing the gap between who they are and who they are called to be.

Ryan lives and works in Omaha, Nebraska.

***

Connect

rnh.media

FORGED Podcast — available on all major platforms

The Foundry Membership — rnh.media/foundry

Redemption Mastermind — rnh.media/mastermind

Ryan@rnh.media

Recommended Reading

These are the books that shaped the thinking behind In the Arena. They are not an exhaustive list. They are the ones worth returning to.

On Identity and Formation

Mere Christianity — C.S. Lewis. The clearest case for why what you believe must change how you live.

The Ruthless Elimination of Hurry — John Mark Comer. The spiritual case against the pace that is killing men's souls.

Practicing the Way — John Mark Comer. Formation as a discipline, not an accident.

On Leadership and Responsibility

Meditations — Marcus Aurelius. The private journal of a man holding himself accountable to his own standards. Still unmatched.

Extreme Ownership — Jocko Willink and Leif Babin. Ownership as a non-negotiable operating principle. Secular framing, timeless principle.

The Way of the Wild Heart — John Eldredge. The stages of masculine formation and why most men stall in the middle.

On Discipline and Execution

Deep Work — Cal Newport. The case for focused, undistracted effort in a world designed to prevent it.

Atomic Habits — James Clear. How small consistent actions compound into the man you either intended or drifted into becoming.

The 12 Week Year — Brian P. Moran and Michael Lennington. The execution framework behind how RNH Media plans and measures progress.

On Theology and Work

God at Work — Gene Edward Veith Jr. The Lutheran doctrine of vocation applied to every domain of ordinary life.

Every Good Endeavor — Timothy Keller. Why your work matters to God and how the Gospel changes the way you do it.

The Unseen Realm — Michael Heiser. A serious scholarly treatment of the biblical worldview that underlies everything in this book.

On Suffering and Resilience

Man's Search for Meaning — Viktor Frankl. Written in a concentration camp. The definitive treatment of finding purpose inside suffering.

When the Body Says No — Gabor Matй. The physical cost of unaddressed emotional patterns. Required reading for any leader managing health under pressure.

www.ingramcontent.com/pod-product-compliance
Lightning Source LLC
LaVergne TN
LVHW100518110826
845146LV00002B/687

9798950671005